MY LAST TEARS

(Diary of a Battered Wife Who Overcame)

by

Deborah Brisco-Harvey

RoseDog❧Books

PITTSBURGH, PENNSYLVANIA 15222

ISBN: 978-1-4349-9248-2
Library of Congress Control Number: 2008933245
Printed in the United States of America

First Printing

For more information or to order additional books,
please contact:
RoseDog Books
701 Smithfield Street
Pittsburgh, Pennsylvania 15222
U.S.A.
1-800-834-1803
www.rosedogbookstore.com

FOREWORD

(Publisher's Abstract)

Deborah Brisco-Harvey's "My Last Tears: Diary of a Battered Wife Who Overcame" is the story of a woman who overcame the emotional and physical effects of an abusive husband.

The author met her husband in 1982. She was fascinated by him and his love of motorcycles. But before long she found dozens of prescription medication bottles and evidence that her husband was sleeping with other women. He beat and choked her, threw the dinners that she cooked on the floor, kicked her camera across the floor, ripped the telephone from the wall, and humiliated her. These terrorizing bouts of behavior could be followed by her husband's remorse. When he brought her a pair of earrings worth nine hundred dollars, she began to believe that she was at fault.

But the author's husband would disappear for days, and she would receive phone calls that ended when the caller heard her voice. She moved out of the house and instituted divorce proceedings. Her lawyer took her money and mishandled her case, and she spent her resources on lawyers who tried to undo the legal damage that was done. She went to stress therapy and even had thoughts of murdering her husband.

Her own inner strength gave her the ability to break out of this downward spiral and make a life for herself. Gardening was her haven from the unhappiness in her world, and her beautiful landscapes were recognized by the local media.

This work is written as a diary, and Deborah Brisco-Harvey's close examination of her own feelings and the traumatic events in her life are open for her readers to see. The author does not shirk from describing the terror that stalked her life, yet her strength can be found written between the lines. The work concludes with a lengthy list of resources and agencies to help battered women that gives an additional dimension to this offering. "My Last Tears: Diary of a Battered Wife Who Overcame" should be a welcomed resource to battered women.

DEDICATION

To my sisters, Cynthia, and Carmen, and Lord knows I can't forget Cousins, Vondal Jr. and George, Jr.: We all became real good friends when we were little, always talking our problems over till we fixed whatever was going on. And to my big brother, Willie and little brothers, Phillip and Herby: I want to say "Thank you for always being there for me—day or night, in good times or bad times. I love you all very much."

To my loving godmother, Charlene Ladner, who has gone through everything with me in my 22-57 years old here in Chicago; godfather, Bert Haury; godsisters, Felicia Haury-Koonce and Celia Ladner; and "play granny," Leola Nelson; my ever-loving soul mate, Anidal (Tony) Montalvo; and to all my friends and neighbors who witnessed the madness I endured and supported me: Each one of you helped me through it all. I love you and want to say, "Thanks for being there for me."

To all the policemen, especially those from the 111th St. Police Station, who came to my rescue when I was a battered wife, many thanks.

To Dorrance Publishing Co. and especially Ms. Heather Curley, who walked me through everything I needed to know to get my book in print, I thank you from the bottom of my heart. To those of you whom I know and to whom I do not know, but you made a donation towards having this book published, I will be forever grateful.

And a special thank-you goes to Attorney Theodore Birndorf for all your help from March, 1994-November, 1996. You told me that I had a story to tell, encouraging me to keep writing, and I did! To you all, I dedicate this book, *My Last Tears*.

AUTHOR'S NOTES

I love to write and I think that was the only way I was able to maintain my sanity for a very dark period in my life. While going through Stress Therapy, I was encouraged to write, since it was too painful for me to talk about what had happened to me and what was happening to me. You will note a lapse in time in my memoirs where I have remained silent, but I hope you enjoy *My Last Tears*, my true story. This is pure reading pleasure—a little sad, lots of pain, utterly spellbinding as my story unfolds on how the court system failed me as a battered wife. But I've grown from the hurt they caused and became a stronger woman for it. The battle was on, and the stakes were high. Everything I won, I lost in the end. But as they say, "Do unto others as you would like them to do to you," and "what you do to someone now may come back to haunt you one day." Enjoy *My Last Tears*. It was written from the hurting heart through lots of tears.

There is one CD and one book in particular by Iyanla Vanzant that really helped me through a lot. I've played my CD over and over. It makes you think about your life, where you are now and where you want to go with your life. If you don't believe it can help you, just listen to the music that tells one great story. I guess the part that meant the most to me was as follows:

> *Tell the truth the way you feel it in your heart and in your soul. And don't blame anyone for anything. Accept your share of the responsibility. Acknowledge your part and your pain, but in the end, give thanks for it all. And share your vision for yourself with others because we have grown in strength and wisdom through all we have been through.*

* *

Special thanks to my editor, Glenda Love High, for helping to make this book a reality.

* *

TABLE OF CONTENTS

PICTURES

A FAIRY TALE WEDDING

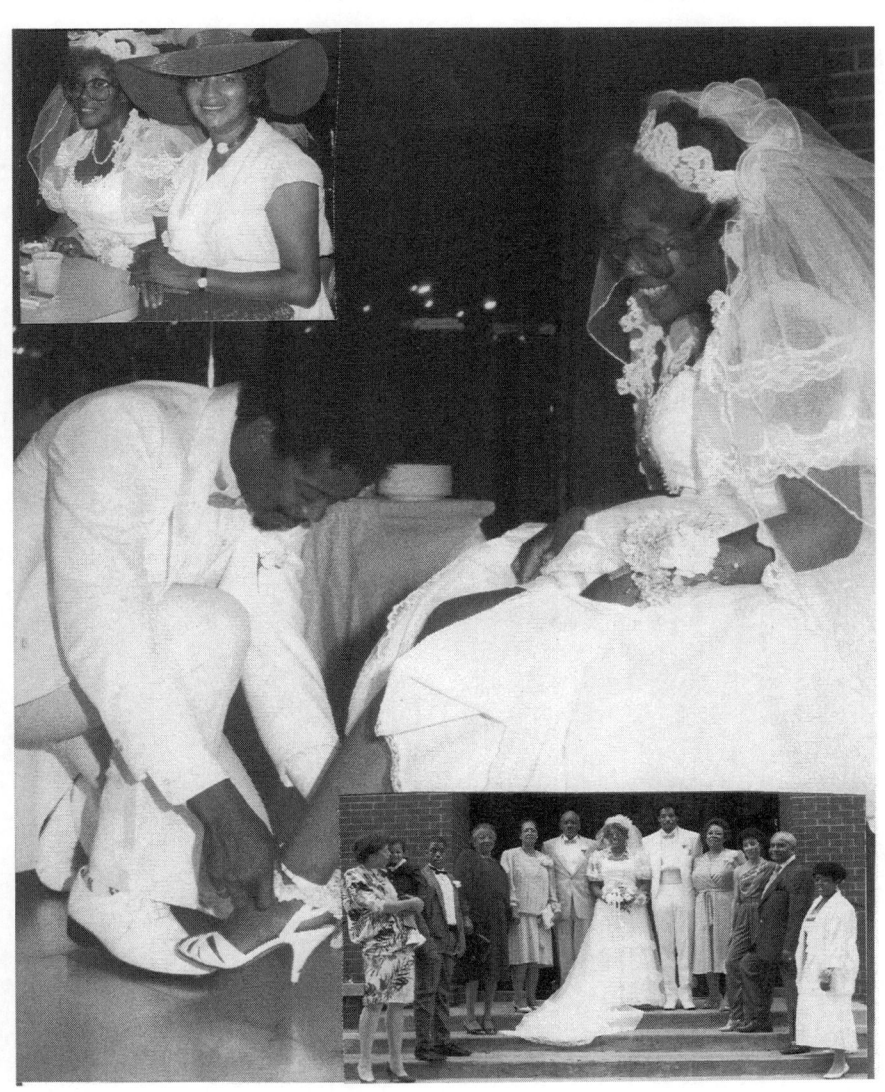

OH, HAPPY DAY! SCENES

PART I -Looking Back

If there was ever a story to tell, this one you need to sit down for, and let me start my true story.

<u>6/25/03</u>
As I look back over the years to August of 1982, I remember how great Billy was when we first met. On a summer evening, my best friend, Deb, wanted to go bowling; so she, her little girl, and I went to the Roseland Bowling Lane. We were ready to start the 2nd game. My little 10-lb. ball I bowled with kept turning over and over in the return slot, which prompted this guy to come from behind the machine to see who kept messing up his machine. Well, I saw the prettiest white smile and big puppy-dog eyes! I think he never looked further than my big legs. All night long we would smile or laugh whenever he passed by. I discovered the guy's name was William (Billy).

About 10:30 p.m. Deb, her daughter, and I were leaving. It was raining really hard, so we called for a cab that never showed. After waiting a long time, Billy was getting off from work at the bowling lane and offered us a ride. After he took me home, we exchanged phone numbers, but he didn't call for about 2 weeks.

One beautiful fall day, Billy called and asked if I wanted to go riding. I said OK; I had no idea he would show up on a 750 orange and black Honda motorcycle! He took me to all his hangouts. All the guys wanted to know where Billy found me.

By the end of November of 1982 I was thinking about moving back to West Virginia. Billy didn't want me to, so I decided to stay in Chicago alternating between my godmother's home and his mom's (where he stayed). We would take off and go to Ohio and West Virginia on the little 750 Honda, which was lots of fun. We had leather bike suits alike, and we would always dress alike.

1

Finally, we decided to look for us a place. I wanted a home, so we began to look for HUD houses. We found our home in December 1983. Billy's credit was messed up from his first marriage; I had great credit, so I put him on my savings and checking accounts and also on my J.C. Penney's and Citgo accounts. Later we got a few cards together so we could get the house. We closed in February 1984.

We had a great time fixing up the house and cutting down trees. We had been talking about getting married. Billy wanted it to be on his birthday, so on June 28, 1986, we got married. My family came to Chicago from Ohio and West Virginia, and we had a wonderful time that day and night.

I'll never forget the summer of '86 when we got the new '84 "Dress Goldwing Bike." I was working at the Babes-in-Toyland School. Billy needed me to co-sign, so the bike shop let him bring the papers to my job. Before I got off that day, Billy came by my job with the big bike, which the kids all ran to the window to see.

I had started a club for Billy called the Rider M.C. Touring Club. I had my little newspaper that I would mail to club members every month. I think about the good times sometimes.

Oh yes, I remember my first engagement ring that I got in December of '84, our first Christmas in our home. Every day I would look under the tree for my ring, and there would be no ring. On Christmas day, everyone would go to Billy's mom's home for dinner, and then we would open gifts; but that first Christmas, we had the dinner. To make a long story short, the last big box I opened contained 6 to 8 stuffed animals, and my ring was under all that!

On February 13, 1988, I had a surprise birthday party for Billy's mom. I love doing things like that. My birthday was Feb. 28th, but I had gotten my gift of Teddy Bears early.

WHEN RECESS COMES

As long as Billy worked for the bowling lane, we were two peas in a pod, but he wanted to get on with CTA. He didn't pass the test the first couple of times, so he came home with papers to study for the test one more time. I loved Billy and if he wanted something, I was always trying to help him get it. I learned the mechanics' book on busses up and down so I could break the material down so he could understand. He finally passed the test. And he got above himself. It went to his head.

In '89 my father passed; in '90 my mom's cancer came back. She had never asked anything of me, even though she and my father put 6 kids through school. She asked me to come home in September of '90 to help my other sister out some; so up and down the road I went. Finally in Nov. '90 came the time someone had to be with her all the time. She wanted me home for awhile. On Thanksgiving evening, Billy told me I had to choose between our marriage and home or going to spend what would be the last 3 months of my mother's life with her. This was the start of everything.

I come from a very close family while Billy's birth-mom gave the 4 of them up to be raised by great aunts. He was an only child most of his life. Well, I called my big brother, Willie, in West Virginia and told him to come get me and my things because I had to choose between my dying mom and my marriage. My brother was so mad! He left the dinner table coming to get his big sis.

By the time I reached West Virginia, I found out my father's sister, Aunt Nellie, was dying of cancer too. She died in Jan. '91 and my mom died on my birthday, Feb. 28, 1991. Billy wanted to come to the funeral, but my mom had said before she passed that if he couldn't stand by me when she was alive, I didn't need him here when she was gone. So I told his mom to tell him he couldn't come to my mother's funeral. From that day on, we went down hill. We tried to make a go of it from Nov. '91 to Mar. '94, but he had changed—drinking too much and running with bikers who liked beating their women. I couldn't live like that.

The last birthday present from me to Billy was the stuffed animal, Alf, and the outfit he's wearing. He's with his bike in front of our home. (Took pictures.)

Here's a picture of me at 49 years old, and here's one of me at one year old on Christmas with my mom and dad.

4

Here's a picture of me and my godfather, Bert Haury, and one of my god-mother, Charlene Ladner, and me in a white dress. My godmother belongs to the Eastern Stars, and we go to a lot of dinner dances. Billy never liked to do things like that. My godmother and godfather helped me through all of this.

Here are a few pictures of our home. I kept a clean home and clean clothes and cooked my fanny off! When I met Billy, he was about 154 lbs., and when I left him, he was 180 lbs. or better. I worked hard. Most of my time at home, I planted flowers all around. My grandmother and aunts gave me a lot of plants. Billy later told the judge he had beautified the yard and that I couldn't have any of my flowers. He didn't plant a one!

My mom always treated my dad like he was special, and he treated her the same way. After living in the city, I found that most people here are for themselves and no one else—not all, but most.

Here is a picture of my god-niece who just couldn't understand what happened to Uncle Billy.

EVIDENCE OF MY "GREEN THUMB"

PART II - Living A Nightmare

Last sex with Billy was before June 30, 1989. None since. Found medicine bottles in trash. Under doctor's care since July 6th and went again Aug. 1, 1989. Still under doctor's care. I called Walgreens on Cottage Grove, asked them about drugs. They advised me to go to doctor for checkup since Billy didn't tell me he had an infection. On July 27, I found rubbers and 10 phone nos. in his wallet.

These were the prescriptions: (1) July 6; No. M281769; Walgreens; 12635 S. Halsted; 468-6202; Dr. Ramadurai; Doxycycline 100 mg; Barr; St 00186; Qty 14. (2) Aug. 1; Probenecid 0.5 gm; Mylan; St 00150; Qty 2; (3) No. 5303209; Doxyclycline; Barr; 100 mg; St 00150; Qty 14; (4) Aug. 1, 1989; Walgreens; 6300 S. Cottage Grove; No. 303207; Dr. Ramadurai; Amoxicillin; 500 mg; Biocraft; St 00150; Qty 6.

1/19/90

After returning from my mother's in Charleston, W. VA, I asked Billy if all his problems were cleared up. I didn't want to catch syphilis. He answered, "You wouldn't know if it was." Well, every time I ask him, I never get a straight answer, so until he tells me, I'm not going to have sex with him. I'm already under doctor's care, and they advised me not to until I was sure he was clear. All month we yelled and fussed toe-to-toe. My nerves can't take much more.

2/2/90

Was a great day to go to work upset with my husband yelling at me, "Yes, I got a bad piece of sex. What you going to do about it?" Made the statement, "If you don't trust having sex with me, we can use a rubber." Well, hell. If he didn't use a rubber the 2 times he got a bad piece, he wasn't going to use it on me.

<u>February 1990</u>
He opened up his own checking acct. Didn't put my name on it. But his name has been on mine since we met 7 years ago. Told me he wanted to start his own credit and things. Well, I was damn mad! But God will take care of him for all the wrong things he does to me. He doesn't want a good wife, and I'm tired of trying.

<u>2/28/90</u>
My table in the kitchen is full of medicine. He claims his leg was hurt. I really don't know. Told me he hurt it shoveling snow last big snow. Told CTA he fell on company property. Been off 7 days. Medicines: <u>Syntex</u> - Naprosyn 500 mg.; <u>Putep AC</u> - Methocarbamol 750 mg; <u>Biocraft</u> - Amoxicillin 500 mg.

<u>3/1/90</u>
Refill on top 2 prescriptions above.

<u>3/8/90</u>
Billy went off at 5:20 a.m., threatening me that I had to give him $120.00 of my money every pay period to make his books balance. Told me to not pay my bills. He didn't care. I told him no. He set the rules; I buy all the food and house things, even socks and things, plus my bills. There is nothing left of mine.

<u>3/10/90</u>
We had a little fuss over money. I had only $20.00, but I gave him $10.00 to keep peace.

<u>3/11/90</u>
Charlene, my godmom, asked me to serve at the church for a couple of hours. He got upset about that when I came back around 4:30 p.m. Just because I hadn't changed clothes, he thought I was going back out. Well I'll be! I did change. He got dressed at 7:30 p.m., left the house, and didn't return till 4:30 a.m. Monday morning smelling like gin and smoke.

<u>3/13/90</u>
My brown fitted sheet was stained. Took picture.

<u>3/19/90</u>
At 5:35 p.m., a friend of a friend stopped me at 95th Street "L" train saying that Billy was telling lies about me to everyone—things like how I wouldn't let him go out; that he wasn't going to give me a damn divorce; and what he wasn't going to do for me.

3/27/90
Came in late. Some girl ran out of gas, so he came all the way home on bike to return with car and gas can. Telling me he did good deed, (but he hadn't offered to take me to 95th Street when it rained).

Saturday morning, 3/31/90
He was yelling at me about a letter somebody sent him. I never did see the letter. That evening left home at 10:30 p.m. Didn't return to Sunday 9 a.m. when he came in talking about my girlfriend and how her dress was low cut with the back out. He was going to take our wedding pictures by her house so she could see them. My God! The pictures are 4 years old! She could have seen them before now.

4/1/90
I cooked a great dinner. 4 p.m. he left without eating. Didn't come in till after 6 a.m. Monday. I think he is trying to drive me crazy or something.

4/5/90
Took picture of dirty tub in bathroom.

4/19/90
Left home at 5 p.m. Clothes on right. Came in at 6:30 a.m. Belt was twisted and 2 loops in back missed. Claimed out with boys.

5/3/90
Left for gas in car at 4 p.m. Never called, came home at 5:30 a.m.

5/6/90
Phone Message: Billy, your called at 6:20 p.m. real nasty. Wanted to know if you were checking in tonight. When I asked where, she got real nasty and said, "Just give him the message; Deborah Miller called 721-9240.

Thursday, 6/7/90
Billy talked on phone about consolidating bills. Needs sis to co-sign. Said he was selling house. Left at 4 p.m. Came in at 5 a.m.

Friday, 6/8/90 - 2:30 a.m.
Didn't come home from work.

6/9/90 - 7:18 a.m.
Still not home. Hasn't called! I called his mom and Reather. Mom hadn't heard from him. No answer at Reather's. Did reach Reather at 8 a.m. She hadn't seen or heard from him. Came in at 8:30 a.m.

6/10/90 - 9:15 a.m.
Left. Didn't return again till 8:25 a.m. (Changed underwear before leaving. They were dirty as hell with bloodstains all on the front. He put them in my clothes hamper.) My sister said I should save them.

6/11/90
I found this receipt #9282 dated today and written to William Harvey. It was from Zedrick T. Braden III, Attorney at Law; 5 S. Wabash; Suite 1502; Chgo, IL 60603; 312-372-3966. Paid $50.00, Balance $690.00.

6/14/90
Left home at 4 p.m. Called me at 2 a.m. late in morning. Bike broke down. Made calls until
6 a.m. Friday morning trying to get him some help. He claims I never do anything for him, but I'm the first person he calls. Calls were at 2:45 a.m. from Hamlin and Madison and at 4:30 from Harrison and Independence from pay phone, 638-9245.

6/16/90
Came home at 6:19 a.m. I told him if he had blood on his underwear, I wasn't going to wash them, so he claimed he had 2 sores. We had a long talk. He claimed he was not trying to make this marriage work.

10/8/93
Left home about 2:30 p.m. Returned Oct. 9 about 4 a.m. on Sunday morning.

10/10/93
About 11 a.m., he left. Returned about 1:30 a.m. waking me up with, "Let's talk." He wants out and a divorce. Then he says, "We'll talk later."

10/16/93
About 11:30 p.m., he comes home again saying, "Let's talk."

Me: "Billy, I've got to go to work."

Billy: "Let's talk."

So we talk again about divorce. I told him I don't want a divorce. My mind hadn't changed from last wk. Then he says, "Why don't you go visit your aunt in W. VA?" Now mind you, I had to choose between my home and my mother and aunt who were dying of cancer in Nov. '90 and left to take care of them. He moved another woman and her daughter in from Jan. to July, '91. When my mother passed in Feb. '91 and aunt in Jan. '91, I couldn't return home to Chicago for this other woman, so I stayed in W. VA till Aug., '91 working for AT & T and renting a 2-bedroom house. I came to Chicago the 2nd week of August. We talked and decided to give our marriage a chance. Will I return first week of Nov. '91? Now, I can't for the life of me wonder why he wants me to go to W. VA for my aunt who has cancer, but not terminal, when he made me choose between here and W. VA when my mom was dying. He told me to talk to a lawyer because he had talked to one Oct. 12, '93; so I talked to mine (who has been on standby since Nov. '90 when I had to choose between my home in Chicago or go to W. VA to care for my mother for 3 months). Billy said he was going to make a move with his life the 1st of the yr. Also we have not had sex in 2 years— not that I care since he got gonorrhea in July '89 and syphilis in Oct. '89. Someone called me in Dec. '91 and told me he had come in contact with AIDS, so I figured that's why he didn't want to have sex with me these past 2 years. He informed me that he didn't want kids at this point in his life and that having sex with me knowing that I wanted kids and after my surgery in April '90 that I could easily get pregnant. On my anniversary (June 29, 1991) I got diamond earrings worth $900.00, so I figured whatever the problem, it was me . . .

10/22/93
He came home about 4:15 a.m., walked around the house and said he would be back but hadn't returned before I left for work at 5:30 a.m. He came home during the day. Was here when I came home from work; left about 8 p.m. Returned Sat. morning 9:30 a.m. I met him at the door. I had been to Jewel shopping, and he was just coming up.

10/29/93
Didn't come home Thurs. night. I left for work 5:30 a.m. Still no show. I came home about
7 p.m. Went shopping at Carson's after work. He leaves about 8 p.m. Returned Sat. morning 7:10 a.m. Talked with his mom, and he's complaining about me going shopping on Fridays and coming home late. I work in Niles, IL. On a normal day, I get home between 6:05 and 6:30 p.m. I've never stayed out late past 10:30 p.m. ever . . . to his no shows!

11/4/93
Thursday night didn't come home at all. I left for work at 7:30 a.m. When he did come home, he wanted to make it seem like I did something wrong. I came in at 6:35 p.m. At work 9 a.m. to 5 p.m. this week. I went early to study new format we had for job. I asked, "Why are you concerned with my times?

I do come home on time every day when I'm not shopping. You come home when ever."

11/6/93 - 5 a.m.
He left for Milwaukee, WI with M.C. Club. We have an answering machine. Never called once. It's now Sunday Nov. 10th 8:30 a.m.

Sunday, 11/10/93 - 12:30 p.m.
I've washed everything but dirty underwear and socks my husband left lay-ing in bdrm floor before he left for Wisc. Made his 6 dinners for the week like I usually do every week, and he still hasn't called home.

11/13/93
This man is trying me! At 5:25 a.m., he comes home, lies down for 2 seconds, then jumps up, and tells me he has to get some air. Shoes untied, no coat, zip-ping his pants as he walked out, got in his car, and drove off!

I went shopping with my godmother leaving at 9:45 a.m. Sunday, and he still hadn't called or come home.

11/15/93
Today I came home, started cooking him 3 more dinners to put in the ice box. I felt sick to my stomach, went to throw up in toilet and lifted top, and his cigarette butts and unflushed feces are looking at me! Now, this is too much for anyone! I'm going to kill this "M.F." one day soon! I threw up in bathtub.

11/20/93
Started to pick a fight over me not going outside to get his clothes out of the trunk of the car to wash. I told him I couldn't drive his car; I told him, "No! You've been in and out of the trunk over and over. You could have brought them in." Then he said, "I'll remember that. Yeah, I'll remember that."

11/27/93
I must be living a nightmare!

He came in at 7 a.m. to tell me he was dropping some friends off. I told him he'd been gone since 6 p.m. Friday night. He should have just taken them home instead of waking me up for nothing. Well, I tell you. Since he smelled like he had drunk the bar, I didn't say anything else. Came back about 7:45 talking crazy. I was trying not to notice because I felt a fight starting. Then he said he was going to get up for work at 1:30 p.m. and he wanted me to wake him up. I told him, "You know I'm going to my play niece's 2-yr. birthday party." Now he's yelling about 3 yrs ago I left him, so why don't I get the hell out now. I'm saying, "Billy, I didn't leave you. You told me to choose between my home and taking care of my mother who was dying from cancer. You know that. I didn't leave you."

Then I went on to say, "I called your mom last night to remind her to call you at 2:30 p.m. like she always does when I'm not home, and why don't you set the clock in the room?" By now, I'm trying to call his mom. He's yelling, "I told you to wake me up!" Over and over he said this.

By now, his mom is asking me what is going on. I was asking her to wake him up at 1:30 p.m. He ran across the kitchen pointing his hand in my face and yelling, so I told his mom, "You know I'm going to kill this crazy man one day." Then he knocked me out of the chair I was sitting in. His mom was yelling, "What's happening!" I was screaming; he was trying to choke me, and I dropped the phone trying to get away from him. Finally got to my feet only to be knocked backward over another chair. This time, he was choking the shit out of me! Finally, I was yelling, "Billy, I just had surgery and I'm not up to this!" He was still choking me and hitting my head on the floor. Again I got loose. Now he's throwing everything off the table. Kicked my new 35 mm camera across the kitchen, threw the dinners I had fixed and put in the ice box for him on the floor saying he didn't want this shit I cooked for him. By now, I'm trying to call his mother back. He tore the phone off the wall.

I thought he was calming down and started cleaning up the mess. I bent over one time too many. I had a pain in my neck and lower back that made me start screaming and crying. I started to make another call. He stated he'd tear all the phones up, so I went over my neighbor's house still crying. After knocking till I woke the dead, they came to the door. I went in and called my godmother to come pick me up and take me to the hospital. I stayed there till 1:45 p.m., came back home, changed clothes, and went to my niece's party—pain and all. Didn't want to stay here. He locked the screen doors, and I had to knock for him to let me in when I got back. Now he's telling me I'm not hurt as bad as I said I am. The hospital told me the next few days I'm going to hurt in places I never thought I could hurt, and they were right— the back of my head, legs, left ankle, the bottom of my foot. I'm starting to hurt all over! (I just noticed the kitchen chair he knocked me out of is broken. The legs are bent. I went to sit in it and almost fell sideways.)

7 p.m. - Now he wants to talk. I told him I wasn't talking because I wasn't going to provoke him in any way to hurt me again. I said, "You were drunk this morning." Then he said, "I wasn't drunk; I meant to hurt you!" He had

tried everything to scare me out of the house, so this beating was his last hope, I guess.

7:30 p.m. - Billy: (Again) "I want to talk."

Me: "I'm not talking, Billy. I'm sore all over and I'm not up to this."

Then he began making threatening remarks: "You'd better stay out of my way because I'll show you how mad I can get! I told you to see a lawyer last month. Did you see someone?"

I still said, "I'm not saying nothing, but after your beating today, I'll see someone Monday. You'd better—you'd better find somewhere to go."

Then he calmed down. The dinners he threw on the floor were plates I had fixed and placed in zipped-locked bags to be warmed up in the microwave any time. He heated one, ate it, and got dressed to go out. (Now he's asking me for something and talking like he's got sense. It's like living with Dr. Jekyl and Mr. Hyde.)

9 p.m. - Gone now . . .

* *

(Battered Women Crisis Hot Line 24 hrs - (708) 864-8780)

* *

11/28/93
Billy came home at 2:30 p.m. Changed clothes; didn't say much.

11/29/93
Came in after work at 4:30 a.m., got a dinner I had cooked from the freezer and ate it, and went to sleep. Still awoke at 10:30 a.m. talking like he had some sense.

12/8/93
Was quiet. Started to fuss about some Tylenol sinus tablets he had bought that I was taking for the pain I was having with my head.

12/9/93
About 6 p.m., a detective called here to see how I was doing. He didn't come home till 7 a.m.

12/10/93
Left about 5 p.m. Came home drunk next day at 1 p.m. demanding I wake him up at 2:30 p.m. to go to work. I didn't have any money, so my godmother wanted me to go with her for company while she catered a dinner party. She always paid me $30.00. He raised so much hell I didn't go, and he hasn't offered me any money yet!

12/11/93
Calm, just stayed out.

12/12/93
Calm.

12/13/93
Went downtown on business.

12/16/93
Didn't come home.

12/17/93
Same—brought home case of gin (1.75 liters)

12/18/93
Came about 12 noon; left 9:30 p.m.

12/19/93
Came home around 2 p.m. Still hasn't offered any money to buy food with. (I haven't worked since 11/27/93.) Left for work 3 p.m. Fixed last dinner for him.

12/23/93
Didn't come home till 5:30 p.m. Dec. 24.

12/24/93
Left again 7:50 p.m. Came back at 9 p.m. to wrap two 13" TV and stereo sets. Left to deliver at 1 a.m. Came back at 7 a.m. Christmas day.

12/25/93
Went to my mother-in-law's for dinner.

12/27/93 - 8:30 p.m.
Called me from work to fuss. Came home yelling and screaming that he'd break my back next time. When he called from work, he asked me about a

divorce. I told him if he wanted a divorce to file for it. He won't and I don't know why.

Friday, 12/31/93 - New Year's Eve Day
Billy packed clothes and video camera and left for his mom's at 10:30 a.m. to work on her car. He left his mom's for Wisconsin and returned home Jan 1 about 5:30 p.m. I haven't had any money since Dec. 18 when I used my last at Jewel shopping. Gave me $23.00 to go shopping with.

1/2/94
About 3:15 a.m. Monday night, he came home in a rage. I had the flu and was cold, so I turned the heat up some to take a bath. Went off about this, yelling about lights on running up light bill. I can't use the phone, can't turn lights on; I guess when he said he was going to make it hell for me, this is it!

I've been bird watching and feeding for 10 years and planting flowers. Now I can't even enjoy the hobby I have. He told me not to feed the birds on the ground, so I have 12 hanging feeders and can't feed in them either.

3:30 a.m. - Billy also told me that when I was in Charleston, W. VA spring through fall working 2 jobs, I didn't have to rent a 2 bdrm house for $225.00 a month. I could have lived in something cheaper and sent him that money. I said, "You had another woman living in our home! That's why I didn't return that Feb. '91 after my mother passed with cancer Nov. '90." (He made me choose between my home in Chicago and caring for my mother the last 3 months of her life. So I went back to W. VA. only to find my Aunt Nellie also had terminal cancer. I took care of both—my aunt, who passed in my arms, Jan. '91 and my mother, who passed on my birthday, Feb. 28, '91.) Talk about stressed out!

Also carried on about how he went off on his supervisor and that 2 months ago, he went to the doctor who told him he had gonorrhea again. He told the doctor he didn't have it but just give him the pills to clear it up. I just said, "You still have that problem."

I went to Jewel, bought a few things, and made 2 steak dinners for him.

Thursday, 1/6/94
Didn't come home from work.

Friday - 8 a.m.
Came in; left about 10:30 p.m.

19

Saturday
Came home at 11:30 a.m. Left. Didn't come home at all.

Sunday, 1/9/94
Still didn't come home. Arrived at his mother's Sunday night about 2 a.m. Slept over there till he went to work Monday morning about 11 a.m. to start new job he didn't tell me about. I didn't know he went to Milwaukee, WI over the weekend. Overall, I had a nice, quiet weekend.

2/26/94 - 1:30 a.m.
Billy came in talking crazy. When he files for divorce, I'd better get out! If not, he's going to make my upper back match my lower back by throwing me out and down the steps. Telling me before he gives me anything in a divorce, he'll kill me and go to jail for 2 years and get out on good behavior or something. Then he went on about I'd better make a list of things I want in the divorce so he and his lawyer can talk them over and decide what they want me to have.

3/12/94
Been out all Friday night. Came home Sat. morning about 10:30 a.m. I was leaving as he was coming in. Instead of saying, "Hello," or nothing as usual, he comes up with, "That must be your friend waiting on you in the gray pick up truck." I said, "No, I don't know him," trying not to start a fuss. But before the mess got nasty, our next door neighbor came out and got in the truck and they drove off, leaving him standing looking crazy. I finished putting my coat on and walked to my godmother's house. He went to Milwaukee. Haven't seen him yet or heard from him. (Monday, 7 p.m.)

Friday Evening - 3/18/94
I left home with police protection because my husband had been threatening me to the point I was scared for my life and for things I had at our home. My godmother talked with Billy on Mar. 21, 1994, and Mar. 22 I went downtown to take out a civil protection order. My order was issued on Mar. 24, 1994 at 3 p.m.

3/19/94
I put mail on vacation hold and got P.O. Box 288636.

3/22/94
I paid $270.00 putting in for my divorce and Order of Protection with Attorney Starks. I went through Civil Court Clinic - Pro Bono Advocates. The police told me to go through Attorney Birndorf.

(Divorce went in July 7, 1994.)

3/26/94

At 7 p.m., I went to my home with my Order of Protection papers with 2 policemen and my brother, Herby, only to find that Billy had another woman in my home. The police asked her to leave. She left in a little station wagon that was parked in front of our home. Billy said he was going to turn the lights, phone, etc. off. Then the police asked Billy to leave. I asked Billy for the keys to the house before he left.

About 9:45 p.m., Billy called the house from the police station, where Officer King asked me about my Order of Protection papers. I told Officer King (Badge 10441) the 2 policemen had read him my Order of Protection papers. 5th District 747-8210. Billy claimed he didn't know what was happening.

3/29/94

About 8 p.m. I went to make a call and the phones were turned off. I went over to secure the locks on the house for my own safety. I really didn't feel well. My back was killing me, not to mention the pain I still had in my jaws. This had been going on since Nov. 28, 1993.

3/30/94 - 12 noon (Took pictures.)

Billy was given this date by the court to come and pick up his clothes he needed. I got there about 10 minutes to 12 noon. Billy arrived about 10-12 minutes afterwards. He came to the house in a station wagon to collect his things and not in his 1984 Lincoln coupe (License Plates VZS 954. ID #1MR498F 3EY 650156, 6/28/55, Driver License No. H640-9255-5183, Social Security No. 324-76-8465, Work CTA 69th Street 925-5619, Ext. 211, Beeper #289-8194, Work ID #14257, Mother, Gladys Eddy (maiden name Thomas) 312-874-9499, 7444 S. Wabash - 1st Floor.) He said he sold the Lincoln because he needed money for the mortgage and that's why he was driving this station wagon. He lied. People had seen him driving it.

Billy was taking pictures of everything, even my girlfriend, Terri's husband. She and her husband had come along as my witnesses. Terri was upset because Billy took her husband's picture and not hers too.

Billy got all he wanted including a red tool box I brought upstairs from the basement because he told the 2 women cops he needed it for work and they wouldn't let him go downstairs to get it. It hurt me to carry it, and I ended up at the doctor's office about 45 minutes later. I went from "no heavy lifting" to "no lifting" for the next 3 weeks. The doctor also prescribed 800 mg

21

of Ibuprofen for pain and Alprazolam .5 mg 3 times a day to calm my nerves. I had already been on Tylenol for blood pressure since Nov. 27, 1993.

4/1/94 - 10:15 a.m.

My godmother, Charlene Ladner, dropped her daughter, Celia, and me off at my house so I could clean up a little and air the house out some. Celia noticed a lady walking around after we arrived but didn't pay any more attention until her mother came back to pick us up at 12 noon when she noticed the lady had pulled her station wagon Chevrolet Malibu (Plates XMT 857) in front of her mother's car and sat there watching us and the house.

When I was leaving my home, my 2 neighbors, Ms. Baker and Ms. Shelton, were out working in their front yards. They called me over to them and told me that they believed that the driver of the station wagon was watching us and that they were worried for my safety. I told them thanks and left about 12:15 p.m. Thirty minutes later I drove back to give my neighbors the phone number to my godmother's home so they could call me if anything happened over there and I wasn't there. Ms. Baker said the lady sat there in front of my home for about 10 minutes after we left and then went to the next block and sat for 5 more minutes before driving off.

Billy had the phone turned off in the house. Now I'm really scared to stay at home with no phone and people watching my every move.

4/1/94 - 7:15 p.m.

Detective, Ms. Stube from Area 2, called to check on me and explain the Order of Protection to me. Her phone number is 747-6404.

Attorney at Law Theodore Birndorf is handling my Order of Protection which went through Civil Court Clinic for Pro Bono Advocates Law Office Suite 1900, 33 N. LaSalle Street (312) 726-7331, Fax (312) 580-0921, # X-552-883 - Battery 11-27-93, # Y - 113944 Assault 3-18-94. Home phone turned off 264-8270; New number 289-8194.

4/2/94

Went to house about 8:30 a.m., cleaned up some more, and fed the birds and squirrels in the backyard.

No problem today. When my godmother and Ms. Helen came to pick me up, they said the police were outside looking around as they pulled up at 12:15 p.m.

4/4/94
Phone company will have a phone turned on in my name April 5 around 5 p.m. (Didn't turn phone on until April 6 in afternoon. Number 568-5222.)

4/5/94
Went to house. Neighbors said that station wagon hadn't been seen since I got scared of people following me and left. I had also left because the phone was turned off by Billy and if anything went down, I couldn't call for help.

Mr. T. Birndorf called and said Billy's attorney will be in court on April 14 or before to get back in and put me out again. Boy, I can't take much more. My mother-in-law called also.

4/7/94
Didn't get a tone sound on the phones in house today on new number. Checked on everything outside. Everything was OK.

4/11/94
I've been bird watching for ten years. I've made a small pond in my backyard. I leave the water hose on slow drip. Today I noticed the water hose was moved and the back gate open. The phone company was supposed to come out today and showed at 9:15 a.m. Phones OK now.

About 12:20 p.m. another stray car came to neighborhood, pulled up in front of my house and sat until I opened my curtains and started taking pictures of them and their car. Then they pulled off! It was at 12:25 p.m. Brownish station wagon.

1:20 p.m. neighbor, Mr. Buzz Clayton, came over to speak and asked me if I knew about the little car that had parked in front of my house and that the people never got out of their car. I told him I thought my husband had had the house watched by people. I told him when I took a picture of the car, it pulled off in a hurry.

It's about 1:40 p.m. and no mail has come yet today.

4/13/94
I left work. It was my last day. I lost my job at Stimonite through Kelly Temp Service today for missing too many days due to problems at home. Dan wrote me a letter for court. (Business Card of Dan Brennan, Industrial Relations Administrator; Stimsonite Corporation; 7542 N. Natchez Avenue; Niles, IL 60714; (708) 647-7717; Fax: (708) 647-1205.

1157   CCG-83-1-30M-12/29/92-315(9)

IN THE CIRCUIT COURT OF COOK COUNTY

People ex rel. _____
_____ on behalf of
_____ self and/or behalf of

DEBORAH BRISCO-HARVEY
Petitioner

Case No. 94D4432

☒ Independent Proceeding CALC
☐ Other Civil Proceeding
   (Specify) _____
☐ Criminal Proceeding
☐ Juvenile Proceeding

-vs-

WILLIAM HARREY III
Respondent

LEADS NO. _____

PETITIONER	ADDRESS	CITY
DEBORAH BRISCOE-HARVEY	705 W 117 ST (check if omitted pursuant to Statute)	CHICAGO

RESPONDENT	ADDRESS	CITY
WILLIAM HARLEY III	12715 S UNION	CHICAGO

Birthdate	Sex	Race	Height	Weight	Hair	Eyes	Social Security Number (if known)
6/25/56 (Required for LEADS)	M	B	5'2"	170	DK BRN	DK BRN	327 76 8465

ORDER OF PROTECTION

4552   ☐ INTERIM   4652   ☐ PLENARY

ANY KNOWING VIOLATION OF ANY ORDER OF PROTECTION FORBIDDING PHYSICAL ABUSE, NEGLECT, EXPLOITATION, HARASSMENT, INTIMIDATION, INTERFERENCE WITH PERSONAL LIBERTY, WILLFUL DEPRIVATION, OR ENTERING OR REMAINING PRESENT AT SPECIFIED PLACES WHEN THE PROTECTED PERSON IS PRESENT OR GRANTING EXCLUSIVE POSSESSION OF THE RESIDENCE OR HOUSEHOLD, PROHIBITING ENTERING OR REMAINING AT THE HOUSEHOLD WHILE UNDER THE INFLUENCE OF ALCOHOL OR DRUGS AND SO CONSTITUTING A THREAT TO THE SAFETY AND WELL-BEING OF ANY PROTECTED PERSON, OR GRANTING A STAY AWAY ORDER, IS A CLASS A MISDEMEANOR. GRANT OF EXCLUSIVE POSSESSION OF THE RESIDENCE OR HOUSEHOLD SHALL CONSTITUTE NOTICE FORBIDDING TRESPASS TO LAND. ANY KNOWING VIOLATION OF ANY ORDER AWARDING LEGAL CUSTODY OR PHYSICAL CARE OF A CHILD, OR PROHIBITING REMOVAL OR CONCEALMENT OF A CHILD MAY BE A CLASS 4 FELONY. ANY WILLFUL VIOLATION OF ANY ORDER IS CONTEMPT OF COURT. ANY VIOLATION MAY RESULT IN FINE OR IMPRISONMENT. STALKING IS A FELONY.

(Definitions of prohibited conduct on reverse)

The following persons are protected by this Order: DEBORAH BRISCOE HARVEY

"The minor child/ren" referred to herein are: _____

Date, time and place for further hearing (if Interim Order):

Date _____ Time _____ Courtroom/Calendar No. _____
                               Location _____

This Order was issued on:

Date 4/14/94 Time 5:00 PM

This Order will be in effect until:
☐ Date _____ Time _____
☐ Vacated by court order.
☐ Specified event: _____

BASED ON THE FINDINGS OF THIS COURT, ☐ WHICH WERE MADE ORALLY FOR TRANSCRIPTION, OR
☐ WHICH ARE SET OUT IN A SEPARATE INSTRUMENT FILED WITH THE COURT, AND WITH THE COURT
HAVING JURISDICTION OF THE SUBJECT MATTER AND OVER ALL NECESSARY PARTIES, IT IS HEREBY ORDERED
THAT:

☒ 1. With respect to all Protected Persons, Respondent is prohibited from committing the following:
  ☒ Physical abuse;   ☒ Harassment; ☒ Interference with personal liberty; ☐ Intimidation of a dependent;
  ☐ Willful deprivation; ☐ Neglect;   ☐ Exploitation; ☒ Stalking.

☒ 2. Petitioner is granted exclusive possession of the residence and Respondent shall not enter or remain in the household or premises located at:
  702 W. 117th ST, CHICAGO, IL
  (This remedy does not affect title to property)

☒ 3. ☒ a. Respondent is ordered to stay away from Petitioner and other protected persons; and/or
  ☒ b. Respondent is prohibited from entering or remaining at _____ 702 W 117th ST, CHICAGO, IL
  _____ while any Protected Person is present; and/or

  ☒ c. Respondent is allowed access to the residence on (date) MARCH 30, 1994 at (time) 1300 in the presence of
  (name) POLICE _____ to remove items of clothing, personal adornments, medications used exclusively
  by the Respondent and other items, as follows:

☐ 4. Respondent is ordered to undergo counseling at _____
  for a duration of _____

☐ 5. ☐ a. Petitioner is granted physical care and possession of the minor child/ren; and/or
  ☐ b. Respondent is ordered to:
    ☐ Return the minor child/ren _____ to the physical care of
    _____ ; and/or
    ☐ Not remove the minor child/ren _____ from
    the physical care of Petitioner or _____

☐ 6. Petitioner is granted temporary legal custody of the minor child/ren _____

☐ 7. ☐ a. Respondent is awarded visitation rights on the following dates and times or under the following conditions or parameters:
  (No order shall merely refer to the term "reasonable visitation")
  _____
  _____

  ☐ b. Respondent's visitation is restricted as follows:
  _____
  _____

  ☐ c. Respondent's visitation is denied.
  (Petitioner may deny Respondent access to the minor child/ren if, when Respondent arrives for visitation, Respondent is under the influence
  of drugs or alcohol and constitutes a threat to the safety and well-being of Petitioner or Petitioner's minor child/ren or is behaving in
  a violent or abusive manner.)

☐ 8. Respondent is prohibited from removing the minor child/ren from Illinois or concealing them within Illinois.

☐ 9. Respondent is ordered to appear in Courtroom/Calendar _____ at _____
  _____ on _____ at _____ AM/PM, with/without the minor child/ren.

☒ 10. Petitioner is granted exclusive possession of the following personal property and the Respondent is ordered to promptly make available
  to Petitioner said property that is in Respondent's possession or control, to wit:
  HER KEYS, CLOTHING & PERSONAL EFFECTS
  (This remedy does not affect title to property)

☐ 11. Respondent is prohibited from taking, encumbering, concealing, damaging or otherwise disposing of the following personal property:
  _____ , except as explicitly authorized by the Court.
  ☐ Further, Respondent is prohibited from improperly using the financial or other resources of an aged member of the family or household
  for the profit or advantage of Respondent or any other person.

☒ 12. Respondent is ordered to pay temporary support for ☐ Petitioner and/or ☐ the minor child/ren of the parties as follows:
  $ _____ per TWO WEEKS, starting TODAY _____ , payable ☐ through the Clerk of the Circuit Court,
  or ☒ directly to Petitioner.

☐ 13. Respondent is ordered to pay $ _____ as actual monetary compensation for loss(es) to _____
  on or before _____ .
  ☐ Further, Respondent is ordered to pay court costs in the amount of $ _____ and attorney fees in the amount of $ _____
  to _____ in connection with any action to obtain, modify, enforce, appeal or
  reopen any order of protection, on or before _____ .

☐ 14. Respondent is prohibited from entering or remaining at the household or residence located at _____
_____ while under
the influence of alcohol or drugs and so constituting a threat to the safety and well-being of any Protected Person.

☐ 15. Respondent is denied access to school and/or any other records of the minor child/ren and is prohibited from inspecting, obtaining, or attempting to inspect or obtain such records.

☐ 16. Respondent is ordered to pay $ _____ to the following shelter _____
on or before _____ .

☐ 17. Respondent is further ordered and/or enjoined as follows:
_____
_____

☐ 18. The relief requested in paragraph(s) _12_ of the petition is *(DENIED)* (RESERVED) because:
RESPONDENT HAS NOT YET BEEN SERVED
WITH PROCESS IN THIS CAUSE

PLENARY ORDERS ONLY

This order shall remain in effect until:

☑ 1. Two years following the date of entry of such Order, such expiration date being _April 14, 1996_ , or
such earlier date, as ordered by the Court, such expiration date being _____ .

☐ 2. Final judgment in conjoined proceeding is rendered.

☐ 3. This Order is modified or vacated (provided such Order is incorporated into the final judgment of another civil proceeding).

☐ 4. Termination of any voluntary or involuntary commitment, or until _____ .
                                                 (not to exceed 2 years)

☐ 5. Final disposition when a Bond Forfeiture Warrant has issued, or until _____ .
                                                 (not to exceed 2 years)

☐ 6. Expiration of any supervision, conditional discharge, probation, periodic imprisonment, parole, or supervised mandatory release, plus 2 years.

☐ 7. Expiration of a term of imprisonment set by this Court, plus 2 years.

NOTICE: Upon 2 days notice to Petitioner, or such shorter notice as the Court may prescribe, a Respondent subject to an Interim Order of Protection issued under the IDVA may appear and petition the Court to re-hear the original or amended Petition. Respondent's petition shall be verified and shall allege lack of notice and a meritorious defense.

ENTERED
CLERK OF THE CIRCUIT COURT
AURELIA PUCINSKI

Date _____

Attorney (or Pro Se Petitioner) Name _Theodore Birndorf_ _PRO BONO ADVOCATE_

Judge _MORGAN HAMILTON_
JUDGE _____ Judge's No.
DEPUTY CLERK _____ MAR 24 1994

Address _165 N CANAL 1020_

City _Chicago_

Phone _906 8010_

Attorney # _9270_

Service by Facsimile ☑ will be accepted ☐ will not be accepted.

Facsimile Number _520 0921_
(Must be included if service by facsimile is accepted)

3.) SHERIFF'S/LAW ENFORCEMENT RETURN COPY   CASE NO. _____

<u>4/14/94 - 9 a.m.</u> * * Court * *
I went to court with my lawyer. Nobody could agree on anything. About 5:25 p.m., the judge gave a hearing to Billy as he asked. I have the house for 2 years under Order of Protection. Charlene and Ms. Helen were at court with me from 3 p.m. to 5:25 p.m. as witnesses.

Billy's lawyer was Mr. Harriston (708) 849-0745.

Billy said in court he lived at 12851 S. Union. The judge told him since the house note was in his name and that's the way he weighs it, he knew he would pay the note because he didn't want his credit to go bad.

<u>4/15/94 - 8 a.m.</u>
Claim #10M06447 - Prudential Insurance Company - Policy 02-0H688456 - Agency Data 835-410-6CH093. Ted Wickinghower; (800) 437-3535; Fax: (708) 572-2629.

(NOTE) June 27th 10 a.m. he called and said he would fax me information. Mr. Wickinghower finally decided I could have the information on the amount that was given us to fix our house on 6/8/93 for storm damages to roof, 2 ceilings, 2 floors, and to paint. Billy told me back in February, 1994, if I got the house, fix it my damn self! Billy fixed 1/2 of the roof and that's all!

<u>Saturday, 4/16/94</u>
Went to Main Post Office. Someone had taken my mail off vacation hold for the 2nd time. This time I put in a 2nd change of address card so mail would go to my P.O. Box starting Monday morning.

Post Office informed me that Billy was the only one with a change of address at that house address of ours, which couldn't have been true when I had put one in on 3/19/94 that Saturday morning.

<u>4/17/94 - 5:30 a.m.</u>
With everything that had happened, I just couldn't sleep last night, so I got up early and started over my godmother's home on 116th and Carpenter. I called and told them to look out for me. As I went down 115th and Carpenter streets, a gray car like Billy's was following me. By the time I crossed to 116th St., the car pulled up beside me and opened the door. Well, I was scared as hell. When I saw an arm come up in a swinging motion, I fell to the side-walk. Then I heard something drop. A lady from a nearby house and the man whose arm had motioned came to see what had happened to me. When they picked me up off the ground, I was shaking like crazy. I said I thought you were my husband. He told me people die in drive-by shootings every day and

NEEDED REPAIRS

nobody ever catches them. The man was only delivering the Sunday paper.

Monday, 4/18/94 - 8:30 a.m.
Called Gas Co., Light Co., and Water Co. to have these bills put in my name. They informed me that William Harvey was having everything cut off and the last reading was being done today.

About 10 minutes to 11 a.m., somebody dropped off a lot of old mail in my mailbox here at home. I placed Billy's mail out on the screen door so the postman could pick it up and send it to his new address.

10 a.m. - Left message with my attorney, Mr. Starks, about how court went and left my new phone number on his answering machine.

(1) Gas man showed about 11:50 a.m., took reading, and left gas on.
(2) Light Co.
(3) Water Co.

The real mailman ran about 3 p.m. today leaving only 2 magazines for me.

4/18/94
Mr. Birndorf called about 3:15 p.m. to make arrangements for Billy to get his bike. I called his office at 4:30 p.m. and told them he picked up his bike at 1:30 leaving here at 10 to 2 p.m. after getting it started. Mr. Birndorf asked me when Billy could pick up the rest of his things and I said Friday at noon. (Friday will be 22nd of April.)

Monday, 4/18/94 - 1:30 p.m.
I informed my attorney, Mr. Starks, that Billy had picked up his motorcycle with Police Officer Perkins. (Officer Car 8386 - P.O. H. Perkins #6760. 747-8210 5th District). P. S.: I gave Billy whatever mail was here. He rode off on his motorcycle at 1:50 p.m. and left the gray Lincoln car parked across the street in front of the Millers' house. (I took pictures.)

4/22/94
Well, it's 11:45 a.m. and I'm waiting for Billy to come and pick up the rest of his things.

It is now 12:15 p.m. and he hasn't showed.

Well, now it's 1 p.m. and I haven't heard a peep from anyone.

4/23/94
I made arrangements with Mr. Edgar (708) 757-7624 to cut my grass every two weeks for $25.00.

4/24/94
I sill have trouble with my jaws. When I eat beef or steak, it's hard to chew, although it's much better than it was in November through December, 1993. It really hurt after my head was beat on the floor!

4/26/94
(Attorney Theodore Birndorf (312) 726-7331; Fax: (312) 580-0921.)

Billy, I think, dropped off a flyer on Dirty Red's Funeral about 3:15 a.m. on his way home.

4/29/94
Billy dropped off the funeral obituary paper from the April 28th funeral services about 6:18 a.m. This time I saw the car as it drove off in front of the house.

5/6/94
Billy called my godmother's home but didn't leave a message or call back.

5/16/94
Billy dropped off the mortgage payment book in the mailbox about 5 a.m.

These messages were on my answering machine: 2 p.m. from Billy's new lawyer, Robert Sawyer 987-1197.

Call came from Attorney Birndorf about 4 p.m. 726-7331. Billy needed to pick up the rest of his things.

When I called Mr. Sawyer's office back, he said he wanted me to write on a piece of paper what I wanted in the divorce and give it to my husband because he wanted a divorce so he could get on with his life. I told him if he wanted a divorce to file for it. Then I would tell him what I wanted in the divorce.

Also my front door lock had been jammed with something. I would have to call a locksmith Tuesday morning to have it fixed, plus there was some junk mail placed in my mailbox along with the mortgage payment book. Billy didn't pay the May mortgage. I haven't received mail here since March 19 when I got a P.O. Box.

5/17/94
The locksmith came about 10:45 a.m. and finished at noon. It cost $95.00 to fix the lock. (United Lock Co. #2340. 11255 S. Washtenaw Ave. (312) 238-7877.)

5/20/94
I called the phone company's information number and found out the attorney's name is Roderick T. Sawyer; 20 E. Jackson; Chicago, 60604; 987-1197.

Also late about 10:30 p.m., I heard someone in the backyard talking. My side gate was left open when they left.

I talked to my play sister, and she will help me move Billy's tires and junk lying on the patio to the garage Saturday afternoon.

Saturday, 5/21/94 - 3 p.m.
Well, today I stayed at home hoping Billy would come at noon and pick up whatever he wanted in furniture and clothes, but to no avail. My girlfriends, Celia, Terri, and I moved junk and tires in the garage from off the patio at 3:30 p.m.

Sunday, 5/22/94
I still hadn't heard anything from Billy about pick up of his things.

Monday, 5/23/94 - 1:30 p.m.
Went to doctor's office and received a little bad news. The pain I have now may be with me for a very long time.

5/24/94
I got one check from CTA. Invoice day 5/7/94; paid 5/18/94. My ID #94D4432. (Acct. 00C49DV)

My godmother, Charlene Ladner, received 3 calls from someone looking for me or Billy, but no one ever left a message.

(Note: Check No. 642328 went out 7/29/94. Ext. 4581 Sharon in Acct. CTA 664-7200.)

2:15 p.m. - I wish these damn headaches would stop! Every since my head was beat on the floor, I have this pain in the back of my head with pressure behind my eyes. Sometimes my vision is fuzzy. If it keeps up, I'm going to have my eyes checked. My doctor said my blood pressure causes it, along with my nerves being shot.

Wednesday, 5/25/94 - 10:30 a.m.

Lawyer Theodore Birndorf called me (312) 726-7331 about Billy picking up his things again this Saturday at noon, which will be May 28, 1994. (Billy told his lawyer I'm never home because neighbors never see lights on in the house at night.) Let's see—Monday, I had a doctor's appointment for my back; Tuesday, I went to Stress Therapy; Wednesday, to P.O. Box and Jewel; Thursday, I'll be home; and Friday, I have an eye doctor's appointment. On Tuesday, I also went to the 95th Street Plaza that morning to put my chain that Billy broke in November, 1993 in the shop. I also put my saddle shoes in the shop. I should be able to pick them up on Wednesday. Friday I'll pick up my chain. Well, at 5:30 p.m. today I have Stress Therapy.

Friday, 5/27/94

Today was a very busy day. On my way home from picking up my gold chain, I stopped to talk with one of my neighbors. Before I could hold a good "Hello," Billy drove up on us, parked and ran to talk with said neighbor. I said goodbye and went home about 12:30 p.m. About 1 p.m., as I was leaving for my eye doctor appointment, he was still out there talking with someone in a Peoples Gas van. Billy seemed friendly, but I don't trust him.

Oh yes, I asked the man at the jewelry store about straightening out my rings. He asked what happened. I said they got bent when my husband was beating my head into the floor and I put my hands under my head. He said no and that I might need to show the rings in court.

Saturday, 5/28/94 - Noon

Today has been a nightmare from hell! Billy showed up about 12:15 and parked at Joyce's house across the street from ours. My sister called to tell me Aunt Martha had passed with cancer, plus Billy sat over at the neighbor's house till 2:30 p.m. before coming with a police officer. Then he informed me that he wasn't picking up his things. He just wanted to check on his belongings to make sure they were all right. Now, he went all over the house including down stairs to the basement.

My girlfriend and kids came over about 12:30 p.m. We were going to take her kids to the park, but Billy took so long doing nothing today, we just ordered pizza and played cards. Right after Billy, his friend, and police officer left the den, the radiator somehow broke around the turn-on handle. I called a plumber who wanted $150.00 I didn't have to repair it, so I turned the water off from the boiler to the heater, but the water still ran on the floor through to the basement. I tried to catch the water in 5 buckets, but rugs up and down still got wet.

Well, it's now 9:30 p.m. The water in the basement ceiling has almost stopped. Well, shit! My sister, Carnetta, called from West Virginia about 8:30 p.m. and we talked till about 9:15. I heard someone in between the house and the van and car on the side of the house. I went outside with the cordless phone still talking to my sister to look around. I didn't see anyone, but I noticed the board we had covering a window had been moved or was falling. By the time I got back in the basement, the board had fallen all the way down, so I put it back the best I could. I think someone is trying to scare me out of the house. Every damn time Billy comes near me and this house for any reason, something happens! Well, I called my sister back at 10 p.m. and told her I had fixed it the best I could but anyone could hit it from the outside and walk in through the window, so I locked the back screen door with the key and I'll put the file cabinet up against the kitchen door tonight before I go to bed. Carnetta will call again in the morning to make sure I'm OK.

Now it's 1 a.m. and the water's still coming out the radiator handle. The basement is totally covered with water. I took plastic covers and covered Billy's stereo equipment so it wouldn't get wet. I shouldn't give a damn. If he had picked his shit up on the 3 times he had, I wouldn't have to worry about it. I hooked up the rug shampoo machine and started to pull some of the water out of the den carpet. Boy was that water dirty! My play dad, Bert, is supposed to come over in the morning to take a look at the radiator and see if he can stop the water.

Well, it is now 4:30 a.m. and I'm emptying buckets of water. My back feels like it wants to drop off it hurts so damn bad.

It's now 6:30 a.m. The den carpet is a little better now, but it will take me 2 days to dry the basement carpet out with the rug shampoo cleaner.

My play dad came about 9:30 a.m. and said I needed a 1" handle with both male and female radiator angle ends and that I should take the handle with me when I go to the plumbing store to get the part. Dad bought a 1" cap that cost $1.31. It closed one spot, but a little water is still coming out of the radiator hole and dripping in the basement in one spot now, which is better than dripping in 10 spots! I've finished getting water up in the den. Dad left about 10:45 a.m. Now I'll go in the basement and try to get water out of the rug down there.

I took another 800 mg pain pill to stop some of the pain I feel in my back. It's now 11:45 a.m. and I'm almost done. Tuesday I'll try to find the parts I need to stop all the water. Dad said all radiators have to be balanced before turning the heat back on. Water is still leaking in one spot. Must be emptied every 2 hours!

5/31/94 - 9 a.m.
Well, my brother Herby will be back in town today. He said he may come take a look at the radiator mess. I called Aaron Heating Co. (238-9064) for a free estimate ($100.00). Mr. Sam came out at 8:30 a.m. and told me what it would be and what I needed. He opened 2 drains on the boiler and before 9 a.m., all the water was out of the system, so I finished getting the water out of the basement rug.

4:50 p.m. - I called Attorney Birndorf downtown and told him Billy was at a neighbor's at 12:15 p.m. when he was supposed to have been here at 12 noon Saturday but came at 2:30 p.m. with the police and didn't pick up his things. He said if Billy's lawyer calls him again, he would tell him he'll get a court order and make him get his things. Mr. Birndorf said Billy is playing games with me and I need to divorce him as soon as possible!

6/7/94
It was very quiet today. I haven't seen or heard from Billy since I received the new paper on going back to court which will be on our 8th anniversary (June 28.) The purpose of the court appearance is to overturn the Order of Protection of Sat., 4/14/94.

6/17/94
Somebody tried to break in. The door locks were messed up, and I had to have the front door fixed. I called the United Lock Co. to come out.

6/18/94 - 7 a.m.
Well, today is quiet. I washed down the whole outside of the house and also washed down the front porch. I bought a porch bench and put it together for the front porch and chained it down so no one will steal it. I hope to put together 2 picnic tables this weekend if my brother comes over.

It is now 10:20 a.m. I'm going to finish watering the grass and flowerbeds now. It's 90 degrees outside. I need to call my brother in Charleston, West Virginia to see about his fixing the 2 ceilings that came down from rain damage. Billy got money from the insurance company to fix them, but he said since I've got the house to fix them my damn self!

6/24/94 - 10:35 a.m.
Suncoast Loan Assoc. came by about the mortgage not being paid. I told the man I didn't have another address for him, but in a letter I received from

Billy's attorney, Mr. Harvey said he was paying the mortgage. I told the Suncoast rep I would pass the message on when I went to court on June 28th. The mortgage payments for May and June '94 were due and also the upcoming July note.

4:20 p.m. - I called Mr. Birndorf, my attorney, and told him about the mortgage not being paid.

<u>6/25/94 - 8:30 p.m.</u>
I still feel I'm being watched. I walked to Wendy's tonight and I saw that brown station wagon again. I thought it wanted to run me over. The man driving parked quickly and ran inside Wendy's, jumped in front of me, and ordered one hamburger. Everyone looked at him like he was crazy or something. I just stood back out of his way till he cleared the counter before ordering what I wanted.

This morning someone dumped divorce papers in my mailbox at the house. The letter had been opened. I'll take them to court with me on June 28, 1994.

<u>6/28/94</u>
I went to court today. Billy and his new attorney, Mr. Starks, tried to overturn the Order of Protection, but the judge told them no. My attorney told me to give the divorce papers to Mr. Starks. Billy admitted he was not paying the mortgage note and was going to let the house go into foreclosure so I would be set out on the street. As Billy left court and reached the doors, he turned and said, "Happy Anniversary; you could wish me Happy Birthday." Everyone in court turned and looked at him like he was crazy, but I wished him Happy Birthday as he left.

I called the mortgage company about 2:45 p.m. and talked with Mrs. Creager to see if I could make arrangements to pay the principal on the house to get it for foreclosure. She said only William Harvey could do that and that he had called in but could not give me the arrangements that had been made with him.

Acct. no. 4246492
Suncoast Saving and Loan Assn
Mortgage Payment Division
P.O. Box 028529
Miami, FL 33102-8529
9 a.m. to 5 p.m.

Written inquiries to
Suncoast Saving & Loan
P.O. Box 7979
Hollywood, FL 33081-7979
or
4000 Hollywood Blvd.
4th Fl. North Tower
Hollywood, FL 33021-6733

<u>Fri., 7/1/94 - 9 a.m.</u>
Billy was supposed to be here to pick up his things. It is now 11 a.m. and he hasn't shown yet. I called Attorney Birndorf's office and was told Billy should be here on time and that I was not responsible if he didn't show and not to stay home all day.

12:55 p.m. - Well, still no Billy. One of his partners, Neal, and his son, Little Neal, dropped by on their way fishing. We talked about 20 minutes. Neal was the best man at our wedding and was shocked we had broken up.

5:30 p.m. - Ms. Rodgers at 005 Pullman District Police Station #16306 wrote something up on Billy for coming so late. Billy finally showed up and picked up his camper to his motorcycle. He was trying to tell the officer why he was late, but the officer said, "Man, if the court said
9 a.m., they mean 9 a.m." Finally the officer told Billy, "You don't listen and you talk too much. Also you need to be on time and pick up your things." Billy did mention to the officer that he sold his car to pay the mortgage payment since the house note was 3 months behind. He also said he didn't have any help, so I called my brother, Herby, to come and help him this Saturday morning at 9 a.m. if Billy shows up on time.

<u>7/2/94</u>
My back is really killing me. It hurts with every step, along with my feet hurting with every step. There's something wrong, but nobody knows what. Everybody seems to think it's just the stress I've been under since Nov. '93. Maybe some of the pain is from stress but not the pain I feel in my back and feet.

Billy came at 9 a.m. Burrell #4051 Officer Ms. Kennedy 005 District. Billy and the officer left at 10:35 a.m. (At 10:05, Billy made a phone call.) He claimed he didn't have enough help, so I mentioned I'd call my brother and some of his partners to help him move stuff on the truck. He said no, he didn't want their help. The officer also heard him when he said it. Then he came without boxes or anything to pack in. He took the stereo equipment, TV, video things, computer, C.B. unit, some tools, microwave oven, vacuum cleaner, meat cutter, can opener, videotapes, and storage boxes. He also took the shelving unit to put the TV and stuff on, a lawn mower, some firecrackers, and a bag of clothes.

7/5/94 - 9 a.m.
I've been up and unlocked the gate in the backyard so Billy can drive in the backyard. At 9:15 a.m., still no Billy. I talked with Ms. Queenie, my next door neighbor, until rain ran us in about 9:32 a.m. Still Billy and the police haven't shown up to pick up some more of his things. It rained for about 6 minutes and stopped. Billy finally came at 9:50 a.m. and the police at 9:55 a.m. (Thomas #14060). Billy came with a woman and left about 12:15 p.m. Two officers came in separate cars. One left after 30 minutes (about 11:15 a.m.). Billy called his attorney stalling for more time. The policeman told him he needed a truck because he couldn't be there all day. Billy kept fussing until finally the officer called his supervisor who came over in about 20 minutes and told Billy's attorney that either Billy should get his things the next day starting at 8 a.m. until he finished or that he should make a new date when he could afford a truck. But one more day was all he was going to get!

When the court intervened, the Sheriff's Department ordered me to sit out in the vacant lot on the days listed below when Billy came by to get his stuff:

> April 18 - picked up bike
> April 22 - no show
> May 16 - nothing
> May 28 - picked up a few things
> May 31 - came to look at things but didn't take anything
> July 1 - missed 9 a.m.; came at 5:30 p.m. and took camper
> July 2 - took station wagon full
> July 5 - took station wagon full twice

Now Billy is naming stuff he wants that was not on the list we developed sitting in court on June 28, 1994. To be honest, I'm getting tired of being nice! Billy also took 2 lamps and things, a knife set, clothes, sheets, blankets, 2 pillows, etc.

9:50 p.m. - I called 911 twice because somebody put a smoke bomb in my mailbox and it dropped inside the front hallway. I called Ms. Queenie to see if she saw anything out her front door. The police came and wrote a Criminal Damage to Property Report #Y300966. I've lived here 10 years and nothing like this has ever happened. If somebody meant to scare the shit out of me, they did a damn good job!

11:00 p.m. - I don't know what Billy got from upstairs. Well, shit, after walking around, he took all the sheets and blankets and my new water sprinkler and hose for the yard.

About midnight, someone was running between the van and the house beating the side of the house like they wanted to scare me out of the house.

7/6/94 - 8:30 a.m.
I called Mr. Birndorf's office and told him about everything that happened yesterday. Somebody got the icebox timer off the floor yesterday, and I've got to get someone here to look at the refrigerator since everything in the freezer has unfrozen now. Mr. Birndorf said I could put everything in the garage and he can get it from there.

I bought a smoke alarm for the hallway by the inside mailbox in case someone drops another smoke bomb in the mailbox.

7/7/94 - 9:25 a.m.
I went to Jewel to replace the water hose and sprinkler Billy stole when he was here on July 5th. The cost was $17.11. I also went to the hardware store on 111th Street and bought 3 chains and locks and paint for my 3 picnic tables in the backyard. (Cost $40.19).

4:00 p.m. - Mr. Starks called to let me know he had filed for my divorce and sent a copy to Billy's mom's house and to his attorney.

5:00 p.m. - Leola Nelson, my "play granny," stopped by to give me one of her water hoses so I would have one, since Billy took mine.

7/8/94
I went to the Imaging Center for more X-rays on my back.

7/16/94
Tony came by to look at my refrigerator, but he couldn't figure out what was wrong.

7/17/94
I had the repairman come out to fix the refrigerator for $40.00.

7/18/94
Since Billy made that phone call from here, he has gotten my phone number. Somehow he must have had Caller ID.

7/20/94 - 2:30 p.m.
Billy said his attorney told him to call me and get information. He called about new insurance papers for medical insurance through CTA and said he needed my social security number, which I gave him. He mentioned picking up his things this Thursday or Friday. When I asked him how he got my phone number, he wouldn't answer me. I asked him a couple of times, and he finally said he had had it for a long time.

Somebody had been calling and hanging up on me. I had put a trace on the calls by hitting *57. Billy had mentioned I was never home and I asked him how he knew. He didn't answer me at all, and when I went to ask him something else, he just hung up the phone. It sounded like he may have recorded the phone call or something.

4:45 p.m. - I went to my attorney's office and told him what had happened. Mr. Starks said Billy wasn't supposed to contact me at all. He said he was going to call Billy's lawyer on the matter. Earlier, Billy had given me his address as 444 Pacesetter Parkway, Riverdale, IL 60627 and his phone number as (708) 841-3744.

7/22/94 - 6:30 p.m.
Billy called to tell me that the guys that were supposed to help him didn't show, so he would try to pick up his things later. Then he asked me why I keep my answering machine on all the time or was I screening all my calls. I told him yes, and then he said the strangest thing—"You must be scared of something being over there by yourself."

I said, "Why do you say that?"

He didn't answer. He just said he'd call and let me know when he would pick up his things. I don't understand him. When he was in court on June 28th, his attorney and mine told him not to come around me or contact me in any way. But he goes against everything they tell him.

7:00 p.m. - Well, people have been calling and hanging up or breathing into the phone saying nothing or asking for someone they know doesn't live here. I hit *57 twice so far today.

7/23/94 - 9:00 a.m.
A. J. came by to let me know the cost of supplies I would need to fix the ceiling that was damaged by rain and wind in May of '93. It will cost about $100.00 for materials. He and his workers will be in and out taking down all the old ceiling so they can fix it later.

10:00 a.m. - I put a new message on my answering machine. I'm screening all calls by requesting name and number and then I'll call the person back. I do not want any more crank phone calls!

7/26/94 - 1:45 p.m.
Billy left 2 messages on my answering machine about picking up his things. He also called Charlene and talked with Ms. Helen's son, Ronnie, asking him about who put the smoking firecracker in my mailbox, but he didn't mention it on my answering machine.

4:00 p.m. - I called Mr. Starks, my attorney, and he said if I make arrangements with Billy without the attorneys on both sides not being involved that I would violate my Order of Protection. He advised me to tape the call and tell Billy to go through his attorney on the date he wanted to pick up his things.

9:35 p.m. - Billy called to tell me he was coming tomorrow to pick up some of his things. I told him my attorney advised me not to make any arrangements and that they had to be in writing through both attorneys. He replied, "Do you want me to hate you or something?"

I said, "No, but I have to do what my attorney says."

Then Billy said I should drop my Order of Protection against him because it would be more beneficial if I did and I could still live in the house. I said, "No, please do as I ask. You aren't supposed to be calling me anyway."

He replied, "I'll be there tomorrow morning for some of my things and I don't have to go through no attorneys to do it!"

7/30/94
I received a printout of all calls made from my phone in July. Sure enough Billy's phone number (708) 841-3744 showed up at 10:04 on July 2nd when he made a call from here. His lawyer's office number (312) 987-1197 also showed up as a 15-minute call from here on July 5th. That was the day Officer Thomas had to call his boss to come to my house to talk to Billy and his attorney, Mr. Sawyer.

7/31/94
Billy called sometime after 10:00 a.m. wanting the damn measurements of his headboard on his bedroom set. I think I told him 62". Then he asked if my sister was in town. I laughed and said no. I guess that's why he wanted to get his furniture last week so the house would be empty when he and his

Theodore Birndorf
Attorney at Law
Suite 1900
33 North LaSalle Street
Chicago, IL 60602-2604
(312) 726-7331   fax (312) 580-0921

Invoice submitted to:
Deborah Brisco-Harvey
702 West 117th Street
Chicago, IL 60628

August 1, 1994
In Reference To: Domestic Violence
Invoice # 10000

        Professional services

		Hrs/Rate	Amount
3/24/94-	court: ex-parte order of protection	2.50 200.00/hr	500.00
3/30/94-	phone call client: 11652 South Carpenter 60643; was served his papers Saturday; is in the process of turning off the utilities	0.25	43.75
3/31/94-	letter client: reminder that court is April 14	0.25	43.75
4/5/94-	phone call client: left message on beeper	0.25	NO CHARGE
-	phone call other: William Harvey has changed number to his pager 289-8194	0.25	43.75
-	phone call other attorney: Hairston *849-0745 will be representing husband, plans to come in Monday April 11 to vacate	0.25	43.75

	Hrs/Rate	Amount
the order, wants a divorce; client has been to Benjamin Starks for a divorce, am I going to represent her?		
4/5/94- phone call client: not in, left message	0.25	NO CHARGE
- phone call client: will contact her divorce lawyer; I will represent her during the order of protection	0.25	43.75
4/11/94- court: noone else appeared, continued to April 22	0.75 200.00/hr	150.00
4/14/94- court: two year order entered for exclusive possession, $450 monthly maintenance	6.00 200.00/hr	1,200.00
4/15/94- court: changed support amount in order to properly reflect judge's order	0.75 200.00/hr	150.00
- letter other: CTA enclosing withholding order	0.25	43.75
4/18/94- phone call other attorney: Janet Mazurek - told her I would cancel my order of protection tomorrow	0.25	43.75
- phone call client: he can come to pick up his stuff Friday at noon	0.25	43.75
- phone call other: Bill can pick up his stuff Friday at noon (to voicemail)	0.25	NO CHARGE
- phone call client: also wants him to pick up his trike, camper, van, car	0.25	43.75
- phone call other attorney: told him of Friday, and that Starks, not I, will represent her in the divorce	0.25	43.75
4/30/94- postage, stats and FAX		
5/3/94- phone call client: dropped off house payment book; will talk to Starks; told her my portion of her case is completed	0.25	43.75

Deborah Brisco-Harvey   Page   3

		Hrs/Rate	Amount
5/16/94-	phone call other attorney: Roderick Sawyer substituting for Hairston would like to make arrangements for Bill Harvey to pick up his personal belongings	0.25	43.75
-	phone call client: told her answering machine of phone call	0.25	NO CHARGE
5/25/94-	phone call other attorney: Sawyer wants to arrange for pickup of personalty; is amending his complaint	0.25	43.75
-	phone call client: has made arrangements twice for pickup; Saturday at noon okay; her lawyer has filed and summons is outstanding	0.25	43.75
-	phone call other attorney: can pick up Saturday; told him that her lawyer had filed a complaint; he will call me back if the time is not okay	0.25	43.75
-	phone call client: is Saturday okay? told her I would let her know if I found out it is not okay	0.25	43.75
5/31/94-	phone call client: Billy was at neighbor's at noon Saturday but didn't come over until 2:30, then with police, and then didn't pick up his stuff, and said he was just there to make sure it was okay	0.25	43.75
-	postage, stats and FAX		
6/6/94-	phone call client: I will handle the motion to vacate, rather than her divorce lawyer	0.25	43.75
6/20/94-	dictate: motion to strike petition to vacate order of protection	0.75 175.00/hr	131.25

Deborah Brisco-Harvey   Page   4

		Hrs/Rate	Amount
6/28/94-	court: motion to vacate order of protection denied	3.00	600.00
		200.00/hr	
-	letter other attorney: re more petitions	0.25	43.75
-	letter other: Starks re his representation	0.25	43.75
6/30/94-	postage, stats and FAX		
7/6/94-	phone call client: Billy came over yesterday to get his stuff and made such a fuss that supervisor had to be called, and he kept taking things out that he shouldn't have	0.25	43.75
7/25/94-	phone call other: Leslie at PBA - gave her status	0.25	43.75
7/28/94-	phone call client: looking for a document not in my file	0.25	43.75
	For professional services rendered	20.50	$3,743.08
	Balance due		$3,743.08

Attorney summary

Attorney	Hours
tb	20.50

Informational - This is Not a Bill

helpers came. He just doesn't understand that I wish this shit was out when the court gave a date in April so I can get my things out of storage in West Virginia.

8/1/94
I filed a police report on whoever is calling and hanging up on me all hours of the night and day. Report #Y349400. Six trace calls from July 22 to Aug. 1. Calls started July 5 but didn't start trace to July 22. Today 1st call and hang-up was as 10 a.m. Then 3 calls 6:50 and 7 p.m.

8/4/94
I was sleep about 7:45 p.m. when Billy called and the phone woke me up. He said he was coming here Friday to pick up his things about 12 noon and hung up.

8/5/94
Billy called about 11:15 a.m. to tell me his help didn't come through and that he was waiting on a phone call in 20 minutes. If they didn't call, he would go to the liquor store on 119th and Halsted and get 2 winos to help him. I think I recorded the message (if the machine is working this time). Billy finally showed at 2:30 p.m. using my phone and giving the 2 men who needed water my glasses without asking me. He took a lot of stuff on the court order list and a lot that wasn't—like a snow blower, ladders, towels, welder and tanks, and goodness knows what else. He also took the new turntables for the stereo system from the attic. Then when he was leaving, he made a smart crack about he's making a list of things he couldn't find and that I was going to be responsible for them. (This makes about the 9th time he has been in removing things.) As he was leaving, he said, "Since you won't let me get what I want, I've changed my mind. I was going to give you the house, but now I'm not."

Officer Fidyk (Badge 17314, Beat 524) said by Billy always removing things that he shouldn't that he couldn't make me responsible for anything. I told Billy a week ago he had to go through my lawyer to make arrangements to come here. He refused to do this, so I left a message at my lawyer's office that I was tired and this would be the last time Billy would be here.

About 10:45 a.m., Billy claimed he had to return the U-Haul truck by 5 p.m. because the company said they had to send the truck out of town and he couldn't finish today. He would be back later. I told him he had one more day when he left July 5, and today was it! I said I was going to put the rest of that shit in the garage next week. I wanted it out of the house! Celia was here with me.

At 5:13 p.m., Billy called back asking me if he had left the legs to his sofa. I looked in the living room and told him no and taped the message.

Also while Billy was moving a dresser and chest out of the bedroom, he left a lot of stuff he didn't want, but when taking the drawers out, he found about 6 pairs of my new panties. Instead of leaving them in the bedroom, as he passed by me, Officer Fidyk, my girlfriend, Celia, and the 2 men he had brought, he reached behind the chest and threw the panties in our faces. I'm beginning to hate this "M.F." with a passion! We all looked at him like he was crazy. The officer said, "She has given you more chances to get your things than most women. She didn't deserve what you just did."

After Billy left, the officer said I shouldn't let him that close to me again. He could have killed us instead of throwing those clean panties in our faces.

8/13/94
Mr. Edgar cut the grass and I paid him $75.00 for the last 3 cuts.

8/16/94
I went to Handy Andy's to pick up 2 rolls of black felt so I could have the other half of the roof fixed. Billy got money from the insurance company in June '93 to do the roof and for the water damage inside of the house. He fixed 1/2 of the roof and told me in March '94 that if I got the damn house to fix it myself. Well, he kept the money from the insurance company. A.J. Construction is working on the house for me.

8/22/94
Kids or someone is still running between the van, car, and the house. I bought a motion detector ($14.74) for both sides of the house. I received a phone bill for 9 trace calls amounting to $39.30.

8/23/94
I finally found Royal Sovereign Hazel Bend Shingles for the roof. Materials cost $118.00 for 11 bundles. Now they can finish the roof for me this week.

8/31/94
Officer Thomas stopped in to check on me.

9/1/94
Alton and Tony worked on the roof. They needed roof cement to seal the chimney. They also had a dump truck take away most of the trash. We couldn't get the trash between the house, van, and car.

9/6/94
Allen Jones came by to work on the roof about 1 p.m. He may finish everything but the gutters. He worked till dark.

About 3:45 a.m., somebody was shaking my back screen door like they wanted to break it down. They also rattled the ladder under the table in the backyard. It happened again about 5:50 a.m. I got up. It always stops when I turn all the lights on. It's like somebody is trying to scare me to death.

9/8/94
My next door neighbor, Mary Murray, told me yesterday afternoon, a police officer was looking around the house and then left.

9/9/94 - 12 Noon
Billy was riding his motorcycle through the alley looking around or something.

I called C.M. Butler Auto Repair, 995-0444, at 12005 S. Halsted, to tow the van and car from the side of the house. They placed the van in front of the garage and the car on the side of it under some trees, so the roof work could be completed without damaging either vehicle. I will see about moving the car and van another day.

Well, it is now 1 p.m. Billy never came back so I don't know what his problem was. A man came to cut the grass, and I paid him $50.00 for the last cut and for today's.

9/10/94
I'm still trying to get used to my new contacts (the new throwaway ones). I still have a problem with my eyes. I've gone back to the eye doctor twice.

9/11/94
Billy's mom had called and told me about her best friend, Mrs. Otis Wikerson's husband's passing. They were like aunt and uncle to Billy and me, so I called Mrs. Otis to tell her how sorry I was about Mr. Fred's passing. She said thanks and went on to tell me how sorry she was about Billy leaving me for someone else and that Billy and his new woman were living together and had been for some time. I told her I wished them the best. Mrs. Otis also mentioned that Billy and new lady had a barbecue picnic but that my mother-in-law didn't go because she was upset about our breakup. Then she gave me a speech about finding someone for myself. I told her after 12 years with Billy, I was not ready to start or jump into anything too soon.

Mr. Fred passed Thursday night at 10 p.m. The funeral is Tuesday at 11 a.m.

9/17/94
Mr. C. J. Butler from the C. J. Butler Auto Repair Co., Inc. came about 6:50 p.m. and moved the car and van to the back side of the yard and side of the garage. It cost $25.00. My next door neighbor, Buzz, stayed outside with me till he finished. (I took pictures of the van and car after they were moved.)

9/18/94
Sunday at 11 a.m., my neighbor Mr. "Buzz" Clayton, said Billy came with about 4 police cars because somebody on the block told him his car and van had been moved. I'm sick of people watching me and reporting back to Billy too . . . on everything I do!

Billy called at 12:12 p.m. upset about me moving the van and car. Then he called again at 12:15 p.m. about me moving the van and car saying I'm responsible for moving them, so if anything happens to them, we'll have to go back to court. He wanted me to call his mom.

At 7:30 p.m., Billy had his mom call me about the vehicles, so I talked with her about the van and car. I guess he didn't hear what he wanted.

At 7:39 p.m. Billy called again; and again at 7:41 p.m.

Monday 9/19/94
Billy called again. I saved the tape from the answering machine.

7 p.m. - Somebody called and hung up leaving no message.

9/30/94
Attorney Starks called and left a message at my godmother's house. I also received a letter. He requested that I call him Monday.

10/1/94 - 4:30 p.m.
Sam from Aaron's Air Conditioning came out, checked the heater, and turned on the boiler ($120.00 cash). He put on a new on/off female angle end with handle; he needed to get 3.1 oil and grease 3 spots he showed me.

10/2/94
I signed up for the food stamp program.

10/3 & 4/94
A.J. came to finish most of the shingles needed on the roof. (Took pictures.)

10/3/94

I called my attorney at 10:30 a.m. to see what he wanted Friday when he called my godmother's house and asked me to call him. I was supposed to be in court Friday and no one sent me a letter or told me of this. I made an appointment for Tuesday, Oct. 11 at 2 p.m.

10/5/94

A. Jones brought a dump truck to pick up garbage from the roof repairs.

10/10/94

I paid Attorney Starks $200.00 with check 0828.

10/11/94

I went to Attorney Starks' office. Billy is trying to get the court to make me move the van and car back against the house.

10/15/94

I bought me a new Hoover Elite Vacuum from Sam's Club.

11/7/94

I signed up for the Low Income Home Energy Assistance Program with Chicago Project CEDA, 224 N. Des Plaines Ave., Suite 101, (312) 207-5444.

3:15 p.m. - Two little kids knocked on my window. When I went to the door, they asked me for candy. I asked them where they lived and who sent them to my door. They ran to the sidewalk looking as though they were looking for someone. Then they walked off.

11/27/94

Do you believe this! About 8:25 p.m. somebody drove a car in the vacant lot next to Billy's car by the garage and set the damn thing on fire! Luckily my neighbor's son came home from work and saw the car burning and called the fire department. If no one had seen what was happening, it could have burned up everything back there. The car was a dark Coup Deville, Plates R6383. The plates had red letters with a circle of red stars to the left of the numbers. I took pictures, but it may have been too dark outside to see them good. The police came about 9:20 p.m. They said they would have the car towed away. About 1 a.m. someone tried to come through the basement side window. When I turned the kitchen light on, the noise I heard stopped. I went outside when it got light and had to re-board the window.

12/3/94
About 11:30 a.m., I went to Handy Andy's to pick up insulation stuffing or unfaced 6" x 15" 480 sq. ft. to do the ceiling in the bedroom. Tony said he would work on the den ceiling next week.

12/12/94
Someone was hitting my window at 5 a.m. By the time I got up, no one was there. For the last 3 days, about 1 a.m., somebody has been lifting up the pool table that is in the back of the house and dropping it. It sounds like the house is falling apart.

12/15/94
I woke up from a crazy nightmare. I dreamed someone had towed the Mustang out of our backyard. Tire tracks were all the way across the back-yard, and they had cut a hole in the fence but didn't bother anything else in the yard. The first thing I did was look outside. Thank God! It was only a dream. The car was OK.

12/19/94 - 9:30 a.m.
The icebox went out again. The repairman said it had a short in it and put in a new timer. He charged $150.00 including labor. It works OK now (12:20 p.m.).

12/19/94
I went by my mother-in-law's to drop off her Christmas gift and then went to drop one off at her best friend's Mrs. Otis who lives over her. She was the one who informed me that Billy's new lady, Julia, would be at my mother-in-law's for Christmas and she told me she has 2 kids—ages 9 and 11.

12/20/94
I replaced the microwave today and the VCR that Billy took with him in July. This was my Christmas gift from my big brother, Willie Brisco, in Charleston, W. VA.

12/26/94
Somebody was trying to get in my front door with keys about 1:15 a.m. After 3 or 4 minutes, they stopped.

12/28/94 - 7:20 p.m.
I came home and there was a note from Suncoast Mortgage Co. (Acct. 4246492) for Billy. Their phone number is (800) 749-7870. I will call them in the morning.

12/29/94 - 11:15 a.m.
I called the mortgage company and found out that the mortgage was 2 months behind. They need proof of the Order of Protection before releasing information. I talked to Ms. Creager. They will send me a letter to this effect so I can give it to my lawyer. I will send the information they need from me this Saturday.

5 p.m. - At this rate with everything driving me crazy, my blood pressure will never be normal and I'll be back in therapy 5 days a week again 8:30 a.m. to 3 p.m.

12/30/94
Somebody tried keys at the back door and then tilted the pool table and dropped it against the side of the house.

1/6/95
I went to the doctor about back pain and a cold.

Alton came by and cleared snow away in front and from the back of the house. He will do the same tomorrow if needed.

Attorney Starks called. Billy put in a counter suit to my divorce file.

1/7/95
Tony came by and put up insulation in the den. Now the heat won't go through to the attic. I bought the insulation from Home Depot. The pieces were 45"- 48" long, 45", and 25".

1/9/95
Mary, my next door neighbor picked me up and gave me a ride to the Dan Ryan. She was quiet. Then I asked her what was wrong. Boy, did I get a surprise! She said, "Debby, you are a great person, but Billy was never no good. All the neighbors here know it. When you were teaching, traveling on cold or rainy mornings, after you would leave for work on the bus, Billy would drive up with his woman and would go into your home like they owned it. If you don't believe me, ask Batena, Ms. Miller, Buzz. Ask them all. You don't deserve this."

1/11/95 - 1 p.m.
I went to see my attorney about the divorce and made another appointment for Jan. 19, 1995.

1:45 p.m. - I went to the doctor again about my back. The doctor gave me new medicine to help relax my back muscles so I can ride the bus more comfortably. Now it's about 5 p.m., and my balance is starting to be off. This happened a year ago after the beating my head took on the floor.

By 9 p.m., I called the HMO insurance office and told them I was going to Trinity Hospital because my balance was going again. By the time I got to the hospital, I was walking like I was drunk, throwing up, and having hot spells and chills. My godmother and Ms. Helen went to the hospital with me. The hospital kept me overnight saying my inner ear was infected again and had my balance and everything off. I have to get lots of rest and go back to the doctor on Tues. Jan. 17.

I got 2 new phones—one for the den and one for the bedroom.

Friday 1/13/95 - 8:30 a.m.
I woke up with hot spells and chills, although balancing is a little better but still walking to my right with a lean. My godmother and sister came over and changed the sheets and things on my bed and bought me some soup and pop.

1/18/95
I needed to get someone over to move the junk Billy left in the middle of the basement floor out to the garage. It had been there since July. I guess he didn't want it.

1/19/95 - 1:20 p.m.
I bought an audio-video rack, which will be delivered at 12 noon on Saturday.

I went to the doctor and lawyer's office also.

1/21/95
I went to Aronson Furniture Store with Helen, my girlfriend, and got a full-size bed, headboard, and frame. Also a friend came by to assemble it for me and move the organ so I could fix the den for the TV and video machine. I will pick up the bed frame and headboard one day next week.

1/22/95
A young man named Fred (995-6763) shoveled the snow and I paid him $4.00. He did a nice job. All weekend, someone has been calling and hanging up on me all hours of the day and night. I got so damn mad! I set my answering machine to scan all calls, but when they hear the machine, they hang up instead of breathing in the phone and saying nothing.

1/24/95 - 1:20 p.m.

I ordered Caller ID for my phone. I'm tired of someone calling whenever they feel like it and hanging up, never saying anything.

1/26/95

I went to Aronson Furniture Store Warehouse and picked up a headboard and frame so I could bring my mattresses off the floor. Billy took the bedroom set in July when he found a place to live. A friend picked up my new bed for me at 3701 W. 47th Place and also put it together for me about 7:30 p.m.

The mortgage company left another notice where Billy refused to pay the bill. He wants the house foreclosed on so I will be set out in the street. My nerves can't take much more of this shit!

I'm still getting hang-up phone calls.

1/30/95

I felt like I was being watched this morning by a man in a car I didn't recognize. It was a dark old model Lemans that circled the block when I left home. By the time I reached the bus stop, he was parked at State Farm's parking lot right in front of the bus stop. I didn't feel right so I stood across the street at Wendy's till the bus came. Then he pulled off.

Oh shit! My jaws are hurting again. I guess one day I'll go to the damn dentist. Cold weather doesn't help my back much. It hurts more.

1/31/95

I wrote my lawyer, B. E. Starks, about the notice and contacts I've made with Suncoast Mortgage Co. I wrote Suncoast, giving them Billy's mother's phone number and address and Billy's beeper number, address, etc. I also wrote J. C. Penney's and Citgo about either getting my name taken off the joint accounts or putting the accounts in my name.

7 p.m. - My mother-in-law called today asking about my health. She mentioned she only sees Billy for about 15 minutes on Fridays.

2/3/95

I received my Caller ID for my telephone. Maybe now I'll see who's been calling and hanging up on me.

2/4/95

I went to the doctor. He told me I had to keep medication on hand at all times. It's called Meclizine for my inner ear and it's used to prevent my ear from going out and me losing control of my balance. This has been going on every since my head was beaten on the floor in November '93. I turned the hospital bill into the nurse.

2/6/95
I mailed the note to Suncoast Mortgage Company.

2/8/95 - 9:10 p.m.
I had just turned the light off in the bedroom and gone to bed when someone began banging on my front window. By the time I ran to the front, I heard a woman laughing, but I couldn't see anyone.

2/9/95
I wrote Suncoast Mortgage Co. again with information on Billy and his address.

2/17/95
There were about 4 or 5 anonymous calls on my Caller ID.

2/18/95
After picking up mail from my P.O. Box, I noticed a letter from Billy's attorney. I didn't understand it, so I mailed a copy to my Lawyer, Mr. Starks.

2/22/95 - 8:15 a.m.
I haven't heard anything from Mr. Starks, so I guess things are OK. I'll call him later today.

Well, I'm still trying to work part time for Kelly Temporary Service, but after this morning, I don't know if I'll be able to continue. As I was walking to the bus stop at Jefferson Park to catch the 225 Pace Bus, it felt like my body was slowing down to a complete stop. As I reached the bus, and with the next forward step, I had a pain in my lower back and fell flat, like a pancake! Everybody turned to help me, and I noticed that everything they were saying sounded scrambled to me. It took me a few seconds to get myself together to answer that my back hurt, but I thought I was OK. Two men lifted me off the ground and helped me on the bus. By the time I reached work, I had a little pain in my back and a large pain in the back of my head. I took one of my 800 Motron pills and called my doctor's office at 9 a.m. I was told to call back at 10:30 and then was told to call back for Dr. Aimes at 2:30 p.m., which I did and told him what had happened. He asked me to come in Thursday for a checkup again saying I may be trying to do too much too soon.

Well, it is now 7:30 p.m. I called an old friend, Mrs. Otis, to see how she was doing. In the next breath, all she could do was talk about Billy and his new woman—how Julia was a teacher and had a sick boy and a daughter. That made me mad. Here this asshole asked me to stop teaching in '92 because he claimed I was burned out at the end of the day and that he made enough money for the 2 of us. He told me I could stay home and do what I liked best like work around the house and in my flowerbeds. Then he beats me up! My back is messed up for life, my inner ear goes out, and my balance is shot most of the time. I can't teach or work with kids, and he's going with a teacher now. I'm so mad I could scream!

Well, finally I told Mrs. Otis I just called to make sure her and my mother-in-law were OK since they're best friends. She wanted me to come over this weekend. I haven't seen them since Christmas, so I told her I'd try.

3/13/95
Talked with my lawyer about the Mar. 15th court date.

3/14/95
Went by Attorney Starks' office and signed more paperwork. Billy and his lawyer are counter suing something. When I came home, my Caller ID had 2 anonymous calls. Somebody knows I have Caller ID now and is blocking their number. Time of calls: 4:50 p.m., 5:10 p.m.; 7:56 p.m.

3/16/95
Called Mr. Starks to see how court went, but he wasn't in. His secretary said he'll call if things weren't OK.

3/17/95
I remember Attorney Starks saying Billy was trying to say I moved in our home after we were married and I may have to prove this in court. So I got a letter together to sign saying this was a tale, and I found on one of the court papers where he really stated this lie. I have about 8 people who will verify that I lived in my home in '84.

3/18/95
(Yardwork front & back) I hired "Emmit" Ronald Jackson to clean out my flowerbeds and rake dead pines up out of grass. Paid him $25.00. He also did neighbor Ms. Queenie Shelton's front yard for $10.00 and Mrs. Miller's front and backyard for $25.00. My neighbors really like his work.

3/21/95 - 7:05 p.m.
When I took the mail out of indoor mailbox, there was one smoke firecracker. There wasn't much smell, so I didn't call police. They must have thought I was home at the time. Next time I will call the police. Talked to my mother-in-law. She's OK.

3/31/95
Emmit came over during afternoon and finished cleaning yard. Raked and took all that old wood and stuff between Ms. Queenie's and our house and put out for garbage men to get. When I came in about 6 p.m., I found 2 more smoke firecrackers in my mailbox.

With people putting smoke bombs in my indoor mailbox, I got scared and wanted to know if Billy had paid the insurance on the house. Mortgage Co. first gave me the run-around, so I finally called Ms. Reddrick at 1(800) 749-8875 today for help. We got our insurance through her in the past. Haven't heard anything yet.

4/1/95
#2140784 - Made police report on smoke firecrackers.

2 p.m. Sat. afternoon - Junk truck drove up in back. Took old gutters and wood that Emmit had put out from between houses. Some little kid was being nosy in back looking at everything they were picking up. (Took pictures.)

4/4/95
Have been having bad, bad dreams every since last smoke firecracker bombs. This morning was the worse. Someone was in backyard with a flashlight about 4:10 a.m. I turned off most lights in the house and stood out of sight of windows. In my dream someone dies, so I'm really nervous now. Then I walk in my den and it was like a red dot following me, so I left there and went in the bathroom till 4:45 a.m.

(In Sat. night's dream Billy was trying to break in bedroom window. In Mon. night's dream, there was a drug war with dead bodies everywhere. A lake was closed by killings. It looked like I had lost most of my family.)

Well, it's 5 a.m. I guess I'll get dressed now. Don't see any more light in back-yard.

4/9/95
Somebody was beating on back door about 2 a.m. off and on till about 3 a.m. I hate to bug the police all the time, but if this keeps up, I am.

4/10/95 - 5:35 a.m.
Someone is playing games with me. This is the 3rd time this dark car with tinted glass you can't see in has done something. Today it was at the stop sign at Union and 117th Street. It tried to run over me before, so this time I wait-ed to let him pass, but he refused to go. I waved him to go. He just blew for

me to cross. To keep from missing my bus, I walked across saying my prayers. I know in my heart Billy is going to make good on his death threat some kind of way. But this car is playing with me.

9:45 a.m. - at work now. And this morning is still on my mind.

4/15/95
Picked up trash between garage and van and car. Looks like someone is living in one of them at night and throwing the trash out here.

4/19/95 - 9:45 a.m.
Verdell Reddrick 1/800-749-8875 / 312-994-5934 for Suncoast Mortgage. Loan #424649-2. Linda at Capitol Ins. 708-499-4090. Ins. Dept. at mortgage co. FAX 305-985-5708. Universal Fire and Casualty Ins., 730 W. 45th, Muncie, IN 46321.

Finally called Verdell at home about insurance on the house. (708-596-1087) She told me to call the mortgage co. at 1/800-749-8875, Loan #424649-2 and ask them. I called them at 11:45 a.m. Shirley in the ins. dept. said they never got the renewal papers. She gave me Suncoast Ins. Dept.'s FAX number 305-985-5708 and told me to give it to Ms. Verdell Reddrick to fax renewal papers to them because they pay it every year. So I did. I called Verdell right then with the information. Verdell said thanks and would get back to me later on. I thanked her.

12:19 p.m. - Phone message at work:

> Debbie,
> Please call Mrs. Reddrick at 312-994-5934.
> Joey Reyes

I called Ms. Reddrick back at 1 p.m. She said she'd fax information, and when it's paid, she'd send me a copy of house ins. policy.

5/6/95 - 9 a.m.
Talked with Verdell. Thanked her for copy of insurance papers on house. She said Billy refused to sign papers, but the mortgage co. had paid it. After 31 days she said the bank would get on him and he would have to sign. Verdell said she'd keep in touch with me.

3 p.m. - Tony came by. Something was burning in fuel box, so he took a look. Said Billy had something wired wrong, so he cut and stripped wires and re-hooked them right. Plus I had him move Billy's 3-wheel trike off the grass to patio.

5/7/95
Girlfriend, Terri, comes over and house cleans every other wk. from top to bottom. Cleaning floors makes my back hurt too bad. Terri also helps me pick up trash outside in yard and vacant lot. Well, Terri looked between the car and garage and called me. She said, "Looks like someone is living over here—milk cartons, chip and cookie bags." (Took pictures this time.) I told her I cleaned this up last month.

5/14/95
Crank phone calls: 9:28 p.m. Miller, E. 708-682-4368.
                              Unavailable - No name or number 4 times
                              6:44 p.m. - No name 312-622-3779

5/19/95
Invoice from Edgar for services rendered: mowing and fertilizing the yard - $45.00.

5/26/95
Invoice from Edgar for services rendered: mowing and fertilizing the yard - $25.00.

Sun. 6/4/95
More crank calls: 7:22 p.m. - Dunn, C. 312-783-2821

6/5/95
More crank calls: 1:37 p.m. - Horton 312-488-3951. Pushing
                              buttons on phone.

Somebody was in the backyard last night. The Mustang car door was open, and the car on the side of the garage is unlocked again. Plus someone tied my water hose around pine tree and picnic table. Unwrapped hose about 5:20 a.m.

Also at 1 p.m. had to see my attorney today about divorce. Left lawyer's office upset.

6/7/95
More crank calls: 6:55 p.m. - Wilkins, A. 312-568-4188
                              9:18 p.m. - Gage, A. 312-737-5989

Wed. 6/14/95
More crank calls: 10:19 p.m. - Dunn, C. 312-783-2821

6/15/95
Need to go to dentist. My lower jaws are getting on my nerves. Something is wrong . . .

Sat. 6/17/95
Went out in backyard about 10 a.m. Somebody had moved water hose again and walked all over my wild flowers by pond where water runs on hot days for the birds. Broke down a lot of my flowers. If this happens again, I'm calling police.

6/18/95
Watered flowers. Nice quiet day until some punk threw half a brick at front flowerbed about 5 p.m. I picked it up and placed it inside on the pool table on back patio. All the firecrackers make me nervous. Last year and this year, somebody put smoke bombs in my inside mailbox. I did put a smoke alarm in that hallway. Well, it's 8:30 p.m. I'll try to rest now. You know it's funny. Nothing really happens around here until Billy finds another reason to take me back to court.

6/21/95
Someone was banging on front and back door from 1 a.m. - 3 a.m.

6/22/95 - 6:30 p.m.
I went out back to cut water hose on. I just happened to look at my storm door lock. Somebody tried to break it out. It's bent on one side. I called and made a non-emergency police call and reported it—Police Report #2279540.

6/23/95 - 2 p.m.
I called Brinks Security System, 1-800-2Brinks about putting in an alarm system. Service Rep. Sandra Barnes, Phone Ext. 2403. Cost $200.00 to install alarm; $22.00 a month-2 year contract. Will install June 30, 1995 at 9 a.m. (Refer. #823236 if I need more information or need to change installment time or date.)

I'm getting scared that somebody will do something to me. I told my god-mother, godfather, friends, 2 sisters, and my brother Herby.

7:30 p.m. - yard work, cut grass. Paid Mr. Edgar for this week and before. $50.00.

Crank phone calls:
6/23/95
8:29 p.m. - B. Feldman - 708-674-7647

10:07 a.m. - no name - 312-484-3162

6/24/95

11:22 a.m. - anonymous
12:38 p.m. - no name - 708-597-8921
1:45 p.m. - anonymous
2:31 p.m. - anonymous
9:20 p.m. - Maya Williams - 312-548-9837
11:19 p.m. - Edythe Rodgers - 312-660-9614
12:18 a.m. - Janise D. King - 708-597-8921

6/26/95

8:42 p.m. - unavailable – nothing

6/27/95

7:57 a.m. - unavailable - nothing
8:28 a.m. - 708-294-0254 - Brinks Security, no name
1:10 p.m. - unavailable - nothing

6/28/95

9:35 a.m. - 708-294-0254 - Brinks Security, no name
10:34 a.m. - 312-783-0626 - Jesmine Turner

6/28/95 - 9:25 p.m.

The funny thing about all these calls is that I leave my answering machine on 24-7 and nobody ever leaves a message. I'll get 1 message out of 5 calls, and some of them are people screaming and pushing buttons on phone.

6/29/95

Somebody was in backyard last night about 2 p.m. I heard them open side gate. Somebody got caught in rose bush. This morning as usual the gate was open, and I make sure both gates are closed before I go to bed. I think somebody is sleeping in one of Billy's old cars or van. During the winter, it was the blue Cougar on the side of the garage. Now I think they have moved in the Mustang in the backyard. It looks pretty clean on the driver's side for a car that's been sitting since summer of '84 and not started since summer '91.

6/30/95

Brinks came about 8:23 a.m. to install security system. Will take about 6 hrs. to do. Rep. Carol Davis called twice to let me know what was going to happen with my new system, etc.

61

(708-294-0254). Installer, George, was finished about 4:10 p.m. During his time here (2 p.m.), strange cars stopped in front of house blowing their horns, asking did anyone call a cab. Strange crank calls. (I remember telling George I didn't feel safe anywhere.) He laughed and said he usually gives a 7-day delay till people learn the system, but he felt I needed it turned on today. He went over everything a lot of times till I felt sort of OK with it.

7:45 p.m. - 312-238-1402 - Deborah Bates laughing in my ear saying, "Oh my, I dialed the wrong number." You could hear others in background.

<u>7/2/95 - 10 a.m.</u>
Well, since Brinks people have stickers and yard signs everywhere, the system works great. Yesterday none of my yard gates were open. Nobody beat on doors or back of house and no strange numbers on my Caller ID. Normally I have 15 calls on it, but yesterday only 2, and I knew who they were. You know, I feel like I'm in a power play with Billy. I'm not going to wait for laggards to test my authority or threaten trouble. I've got to make it crystal clear I mean business. I don't intend to give up something of value for nothing. I've been through too much this past 2 yrs. I need a place to live, and I'm not hesitating anymore. I'm going to start finding time to fix my home back the way I want it. Yes, Mr. Billy Harvey, you took everything out of here, but friends have pitched in and given me a lot, and now it's starting to look like home again!

<u>7/4/95 - 10:30 a.m.</u>
Light on back of house almost came off. Rained hard and windy. Had to have someone fix floodlight on back of house.

<u>7/6/95</u>
Two unavailable calls: 7:58 a.m. and 11:26 p.m.

<u>7/7/95</u>
Lawnman cut grass. $25.00. Two phone calls from Denson Gray: 12:29 p.m. and 12:50 p.m. 312-264-2059. I don't know him.

<u>7/9/95</u>
6:30 p.m. 312-286-6602 - Martin Krpar

<u>7/13/95</u>
7:54 p.m. 312-233-0732 - Raynaldo Veldez

<u>7/14/95</u>
4:11 p.m. 312-568-4448 - Francis Parker

7/15/95
4:11 p.m. 312-995-8805 - Sterli Holloway

6:30 p.m. - Tony put in air conditioner in kitchen.

7/16/95
Somebody by the name of Rick has been calling my godmother's home for me all week all hours of the day and night. Well, he called today at 6 a.m. Enough is enough! Charlene Ladner asked what he wanted, and he left a phone number: 312-734-5768. I called once, but he was out. I finally called again at 9:38 a.m., and a woman called him to the phone. He claimed I met him at the beach with my girlfriends. I told him somebody played a trick on him because it wasn't me and not to call my godmother's home again. The he said, "If it wasn't you, then tell me about yourself. I want to know you." I said, "I'm sorry, but I'm not the one," and hung up. I dialed *67 so my number wouldn't show up on their Caller ID if they had one.

7/17/95
7:05 p.m. 312-624-1549 - Arlista Jackson

7/18/95
1:45 a.m. I heard something hit my side window and then this loud noise on my front porch. I waited about 10 minutes and looked out. It was a Sun Burst rocket. I took pictures of it and kept the empty shell.

Crank calls on answering machine and numbers on Caller ID:
        10:08 a.m. 312-821-4626 - Loeita Taylor
        12:35 p.m. 312-660-1632 - Earlene Ratliff

7/19/95
7:13 a.m. - Curt Zulfer - 708-339-3647

7/20/95
9:19 a.m. - Clara Southgate - 708-779-9345
12:25 p.m. - anonymous call

7/20/95
8:32 a.m. - Mattie Bloodsaw - 312-737-4475

7/21/95
Barbecue today. I tried for one more time to eat steak and ribs, but my lower jaw just doesn't line up after I chew anything tough too long. I'll just take an 800 mg pain pill and eat hot dogs and hamburgers today.

7/23/95
7:46 a.m. - Mattie Bloodsaw - 312-737-4475

7/24/95 - 11:30 a.m.
Went to Saxon and bought paint to do front hallway, bathroom, kitchen, and back hall to basement. Spent $99.20.

Also mailed Attorney Starks household costs and my bills, etc. for pre-divorce coming up.

It's amazing when I'm home all day nobody calls with crank calls.

7/25/95 - 5 p.m.
Went to Stress Therapy.

7/26/95
5:21a.m. - Mattie Bloodsaw - 312-737-4475
7:25 a.m. - Unavailable - Just music playing
11:58 a.m. - Vivia Whitehead - 708-597-4546

(Took pictures before and after.) 7:30 p.m. - A.J. came over to help me paint 2 halls, kitchen, and bathroom. Didn't finish. Left late.

7/27/95 - 7 p.m.
Borrowed Mr. Baker's ladder. A.J. came over to help paint. Still didn't finish. These rooms haven't been painted in 11 years.

7/28/95 - 6:30 p.m.
Tony came over and fixed 2 hall lights and put up new light fixture in kitchen. Had to take old down.

7/29/95
A.J. came to finish painting and help me move bar in basement.

8/3/95
Lawnman cut grass. $25.00.

Went to Stress Therapy. Bad day at therapy . . .

8/5/95
Calls on Caller ID:
       11:39 a.m. - Vivia Whitehead - 708-597-4546
       6:05 p.m. - Vivia Whitehead - 708-597-4546

10:15 p.m. - unavailable - no nothing
10:17 p.m. - unavailable - no nothing
10:29 p.m. - unavailable - no nothing
10:31 p.m. - I dialed Star 69 and called the person back. This man answered phone laughing, so I said, "Sir, did you just call my home 3 times only letting the phone right once and hanging up?"

"So what if I did. Who are you?"

I said, "Please stop playing on the phone and don't call my number anymore."

Then he got smart. "Well, how did you get my number?"

I said, "I dialed Star 69 call back."
Then he hung up and didn't call back.

<u>8/6/95 - 8:30 a.m.</u>
Telephone man came to fix bedroom jack.

2:38 p.m. - Officer Thomas stopped by to check on me. Billy acted like a jackass last yr. Most of the officers stop to check on me. They're nice.

<u>8/7/95</u>
Calls:
>> 10:02 a.m. - unavailable
>> 11:31 a.m. - 312-721-3842 - Eveline Burrell
>> 12:19 p.m. - unavailable - 312-978-2040

<u>8/28/95 - 4:34 p.m.</u>
Marie King - 312-874-8820

<u>8/29/95</u>
Anonymous calls 2:19 p.m. and 2:54 p.m.

<u>8/30/95</u>
Anonymous calls 2:08 p.m. and 2:27 p.m.

<u>9/1/95</u>
Yardman cut grass and fertilized. $50.00.

Anonymous call 4:10 p.m. Then about 11:34 p.m. somebody called acting crazy on the phone. Caller ID showed Willie Long D. J. 312-471-0603.

<u>9/5/95 - 6:05 p.m.</u>
I went to Wendy's for a salad. On returning home, there was an old brown station wagon with no plates parked in front of my home. Someone was watching me. It made me remember Billy telling me, "There is always a way of getting someone out of your life. Drive-by shootings happen all the time." I was scared as I walked on the front porch. They stayed there about 10 mins. looking this away and then sped off like crazy!

<u>9/6/95</u>
Had therapy group today 5:30 p.m. Group was nice as always.

I checked my Caller ID. I had 7 phone calls. I went to my bedroom to check answering machine. As usual, no messages. Calls listed below:

> 9:47 a.m. - unavailable name - 312-481-3178
> 10:34 a.m. - unavailable - nothing
> 10:39 a.m. - unavailable - nothing
> 11:03 a.m. - anonymous call
> 1:19 p.m. - unavailable name - 312-995-0858
> 1:23 p.m. - unavailable - nothing
> 1:30 p.m. - unavailable - nothing

7 p.m. - I dialed Star 69 to last caller but nobody answered phone. This is really scary—7 calls but not one message on answering machine.

<u>9/11/95</u>
Well, my godsister, Celia Ladner, called at 7:18 p.m. to tell me a brown station wagon was parked across from her house. She said it looked like the same one that was watching me and the house a year ago. She said it was driven by same bushy headed woman. When she started watching her back, she pulled off about 7:35 p.m.

Calls:
> 9/8/95 - 5:46 p.m. 312-233-8480 - University Hospital
>
> 9/11/95 - 3:06 p.m. 312-264-8107 - Randi Blanden
>
> 9/13/95 - 9:33 a.m. 312-264-4070 - Belinda Hill

<u>9/12/95</u>
About 1:45 a.m. somebody was beating on the side of the house like a mad crazy person for about 2 minutes. I couldn't go back to sleep. (This hadn't happened in a long time now.)

Group therapy was OK today.

9/14/95
    3:06 p.m. - Unavailable
    7:37 p.m. - 708-862-1234 - Tristate Kirby

9/15/95
Lawnman did yard work. $25.00. Bathroom switch finally went out. Tony put in new switch but couldn't get plug to work. Will need to return and see what's wrong with switch on other side of wall in kitchen.

Sun. 9/17/95
Caller ID Calls:
    3:03 p.m. 312-264-4070 - Belinda Hill

9/18/95
Attorney Starks called at 10:30 a.m. (312-995-7900).

9/19/95
Returned call to Attorney Starks at 10:30 a.m., but his secretary asked me to call back about noon. She didn't know what he wanted. Called back at 12:45 p.m. but nobody was in office. Left number where I could be reached.
Made workout area in basement. (Took pictures.)

Mon. 9/25/95 - 4:01 a.m.
Well, last night was a rough one. I dreamed I was in a hospital with a total breakdown, and my dead sister, Cynthia, came to my rescue; we ran away to this boarded up old home, which we turned into a nice place to live. The hospital didn't know where I was for months. Then my sister took in this sick older lady who was under the same doctors I was, and they would come out and see how she was doing. I would run in the closet so they wouldn't see me. In my dream, they wanted to transplant something in my brain to make me not afraid or scared of everything. I tried to tell them if I wasn't on so much medicine, I'd get better. By me running away, I had proven that. Now this made some doctor mad, and they finally found where I was and started to scare me so I'd crack up all over again. This one Sat. morning about 6 a.m., they started throwing things through the windows. I was like on the 2nd floor. Knocking the window screens out didn't run me out. By this time, news people were outside with cameras trying to get them to leave me alone. Then they started throwing large logs and small log pieces in the house. I did get scared, but in the end, I started to fight back saying I wasn't crazy—they were, and I started throwing the small logs out the window at them, and people started to cheer. If I had to die in this house, I wasn't

going down without a hell of a fight. And then I woke up. It's now 4:36 a.m. and I can't get this dream out of my head. Maybe I'll tell it in therapy today. I think I'm ready for this divorce fight now, and this is my body's way of saying it.

Went to Stress Therapy. Also mailed Attorney Starks doctor's papers and new work sheet. Sheet for Oct. - Dec. - P.T. work $6.75 hr. For new assignment, 4 hrs a day, 3 days or 2 days a wk., maybe more if needed.

9/26/95 - 6:30 p.m.
I screened all of my phone calls through Caller ID or answering machine. Too many crank calls.

>   8:33 a.m. - Catherine Dunn - 312-783-2821
>   1:58 p.m. - unavailable

As I look back over past phone calls looking for a pattern in calls, I found this:

>   Sun. 6/4 - 7:22 p.m. - Catherine Dunn - 312-783-2821
>   Wed. 6/14 - 10:19 p.m. - Catherine Dunn - 312-783-2821
>   Tues. 9/26 - 8:33 a.m. - Catherine Dunn - 312-783-2821
>
>   Wed. 9/13 - 9:33 a.m. - Belinda Hill - 312-264-4070
>   Sun. 9/17 - 3:03 p.m. - Belinda Hill - 312-264-4070
>   Sun. 10/8 - 2:10 p.m. - Belinda Hill - 312-264-4070
>
>   Fri. 7/21 - 8:32 a.m. - Mattie Bloodsaw - 312-737-4475
>   Sun. 7/23 - 7:46 a.m. - Mattie Bloodsaw - 312-737-4475
>   Wed. 7/26 - 5:21 a.m. - Mattie Bloodsaw - 312-737-4475
>
>   Wed. 7/26 - 11:58 a.m. - Vivia Whitehead - 708-597-4546
>   Sat. 8/5 - 11:39 a.m. and 6:05 p.m.- Vivia Whitehead - 708-597-4546

9/27/95 - 4:45 p.m.
My godmother said that same brown station wagon was parked in front of her house this morning.

Screened all phone calls today. Caller ID had 9 calls, and my answering machine is always on. I picked up on 2 calls.

>   5:01 a.m. - my godmother called
>   Unavailable - no name or number:

9:21 a.m., 9:54 a.m., 11:54 a.m., 1:34 p.m.

1:52 p.m. - Joyce called - 312-785-6221 - no therapy today. Ms. Watts' husband has cancer, and she took him to hospital today. Wk. 708-364-1069.

Unavailable:

2:05 p.m., 2:46 p.m., 4:25 p.m.

I dialed *69 back to see who would answer the phone. All it would say is "Calls can't go through."

9/28/95 - 5:05 p.m.

Nothing on answering machine. Phone rang all day.

     Unavailable: 9:55 a.m., 2:23 p.m., 3:37 p.m.

     4:35 p.m. - J. T. Walker - 312-568-5787.

They listened to my nasty speech on answering machine and hung up. I waited for 30 minutes and "Star 69ed" the last call. A woman answered. I asked for Mr. Walker and before I could finish, she started fussing. I said, "Look Miss. I'm checking calls on my Caller ID."

"Well, somebody must have dialed by mistake." I said, "Fine. I'm not upset, but you sure are. Have a nice evening," and I hung up.

9/29/95

Caller ID Numbers:

     8:19 a.m. - Highland Commun - 312-928-6800

     12:04 p.m. - unavailable

     12:38 p.m., 1:26 p.m., 2:24 p.m., 4:06 p.m., 6:05 p.m. - and nobody left a message on my answering machine.

7:15 p.m. - My niece from W. VA. called and left message to call her back. I was outside in backyard when she called. My great niece, Tish, was in the hospital.

10/1/95

1:47 p.m. - Joann Green - 312-233-9464. I let the phone ring twice so the number would show up on Caller ID. When I did answer, as always, music playing and laughter. I said, "Hello," 3 or 4 times. I hung up after a few minutes.

10/4/95

Calls:

     Unavailable, no information on Caller ID:

     11 a.m., 1:38 p.m., 2:19 p.m., 3:31 p.m., 4:22 p.m.

Anonymous call: 12:31 p.m.

<u>10/6/95</u>
Phone hasn't rung once today. When I'm home all day, it never does. I'm still having problems with my jaw off and on. Started Nov. 27, 1993 when I chew. Made appt. with dentist for today at 10:30 a.m. My last full x-rays of my mouth was May '93. This time Dr. Knowles wanted to know why my teeth were chipped in odd places. I told him it was because of the beating my head took on the floor Nov. 27, 1993. My teeth keep hitting together. He said I was lucky it didn't cause more damage. Now I've got to redo gum treatment like in May '93. Then Dr. Knowles will repair filling and chipped teeth. He laughed and said, "I hope you left him. Next time you could lose teeth instead of just chipping . . . ." I asked him about the pain I have when I chew. He said in time it would clear up.

<u>10/8/95</u>
Terri came over to clean house. ($20.00)

Caller ID Calls: 2:10 p.m. - Belinda Hill - 312-264-4070. I called her back after she hung up on me. After I said hello 2 or more times, she claimed she didn't know who dialed my number. I told her, "It's funny you call my home all the time to know nothing." She laughed and hung up.

<u>10/9/95</u>
Dentist's Office 10:30 a.m.

<u>10/13/95</u>
Calls:
12:45 p.m. - 312-995-7900 - Starks Association and left message on answering machine. They hope I could find my way to the courthouse by 2 p.m. today about divorce. Call - no message 12:49 p.m.

4:54 p.m. - Call again. Case was dismissed for Warner something. Counter claim for Billy Oct. 23.

<u>10/14/95 - 10:57 a.m.</u>
Mr. Starks called very upset from 312-374-0644, Colfax Cleaners returning my call I left him last night after 8 p.m. when I came home and played the message he had left for me. By the way, I still have the messages on tape. He was upset because I have run out of money and couldn't pay him anything. Wants me in his office Monday afternoon to discuss case. Needs $60.00 to re-instate my case. He and Billy's lawyer want me to back down from what I want in my divorce settlement. I will be in my attorney's office Monday after-

noon. Borrow money from Helen Harris.

11:30 a.m. - Junk man came round asking about old car and van. (Strange looking, skinny man, driving little gray car.) I told him they belong to my husband.

10/16/95 - 11:45 a.m.
Went to lawyer's office to give him $60.00 to re-instate something Billy and his lawyer had undone. We will have Pre-Divorce Oct. 23, 9:30 a.m.

Went to Stress Therapy at 5 p.m. Meeting was 2 hrs.

10/20/95
Well, I'm really stressed out over Monday. Went to work today. Had a nice day. Got all the way home from Niles, IL to 87th St. before I realized I left my house key at the job. My girlfriend I ride with was screaming, "You are kidding!"

I'm screaming, "We gotta go back!"

She's screaming, "But my 6:30 p.m. hair appointment"!

Then she laughed for awhile. She agreed to drive me back after her hair appointment. She started singing this happy song. I said joking and laughing, "What the hell are you so happy about? I'm going crazy, still looking in this damn big purse looking for my keys—praying that I find them."

So when we got to the Arch Hairdresser on 85th & Stony, I called Peggy at home and told her to meet me at the job so I could get my keys. She took my phone no. there, and then called the job to see if anyone stayed late. The big boss was there, so he left my keys outside in the corner of the flowerbed for me. After filling up Laura's tank, we finally got home at 11 p.m. I called Peggy and told her I got my keys. She told me to calm down and everything would be OK Monday. Then I called Laura's mother and told her she was on her way home.

Tomorrow is Saturday - Dentist appointment 10:30 a.m. and a man is coming to fix the kitchen stove. Now I guess I'll try to get some sleep. Hope no one lifts pool table off the back of the house and drops it like they did the past 2 nights. It sounds like the house is falling down and scares the shit out of me until I finally go back to sleep.

10/21/95 - 4:10 a.m.
Something tripped Zone 4 in the basement. Brinks called 4:13 a.m. I asked for police. They came 5 minutes later. Everything looked fine. They went

downstairs and looked all around and checked outside. Nobody knows what tripped the basement motion detector. I talked with police. They said it could have been electrical. Brinks said it may have been a rat or something in basement. Well, I left back light on in yard, basement light on, locked door from basement to kitchen, and all lights on upstairs.

4:49 a.m. - Now that's a hell of a way to be woke up! It's raining outside. Well, my nerves are shot to hell now!

Sun. 10/22/95 - 5:50 a.m.
Something tripped Zone 4 in basement again. It must be a rat or something. Just finished talking to Brinks.

10/23/95 - 7:15 a.m.
Celia and I met up at 7:30 a.m. to go to court today at Daley Center 9:30 a.m., Rm 2102 for my Pre-Divorce meeting. Court Dec. 8 at 2 p.m. Rm 2102 (Mrs.) Judge Dickler.

10/25/95 - 11 a.m.
Has been very quiet. No phone calls. Junk man came around asking about old car and van on side of garage. I told him they are not for sale.

10/30/95 - 9 a.m.
Some junk man came by and stayed in back of garage too long, so I went out back to see. Well, hell, he was going to tow Billy's junk car and van off. When I told him they belong to my husband, he said, "They're ticketed to be towed." I said, "Where?" Then I said, "Well, let them have it, but you don't take them." (I took pictures.) They were ticketed Oct. 26, 1995 by D. Lainhanm or something. Investigator Star #11679. Car and van pickup date Nov. 2, 1995. (Short man driving brownish van.)

10/31/95 - 7 a.m.
"Happy Nightmare Halloween" - I woke up to find Billy's van and car were gone. I called police and talked with Officer Harrington #18425, non emerg. number 746-6000. I called 911, but they gave me that last number to call. The last I saw of the vehicles was when I came back from therapy and turned the water off in bird pond, took 800 mg and went to sleep. Police Reports for Van - 2515715 and Car - 2515716. I called neighbors, but they heard nothing. Mr. Willie - 264-8522, Vince Baker - 928-0942, Ms. Queenie - 264-4286, Buzz - 568-8679, Mrs. Eddy - 874-9499 (mother-in-law). I called my mother-in-law, and she said she didn't think Billy had got them, but she would tell him what happened.

Neighbor, Buzz, came over about 9:07 a.m. to see if I was OK. He said somebody broke into Ms. Shelby's house, Ms. Miller's car, and stole his license plates from his car twice—all this in the last two wks., and now Billy's car and van were gone.

Went to pick up new eyeglasses about 10:30 a.m. on 111th & Troy. Well, hell, they gave me the wrong pair. The nurse told the doctor he may have the wrong ones. He replied, "I've been doing this a long time" and told me I had to wear the new ones to get used to them. Well, by the time I got home, I had a headache, so I called them back. Sure enough, they were the wrong ones. I told them this was a day from hell and I was not going from 117th & Halsted to 111th & Troy again today. Maybe next wk. So I'll just wear my old ones.

Well, it's 7:30 p.m. and I haven't heard from Billy or his mom. I thought by now he would have called with the information I need to give to the police for his van and car.

Had about 75 trick-or-treaters tonight. Gave out candy caramel apples and bubble gum.

* *

REFLECTIONS Oct. '95
"My Wedding Rings"

Love really hurts sometimes . . . . People always ask, "Why do you still wear them?" I pause for a second and catch my breath; then I say, "Never to remember the good it had, only to remember not to trust that way ever again." For I remember the hurt it brought when I had to choose between the man I loved with all my heart and the woman I loved more—my mom. He made me do this, and she had only 3 mos. to live. I destroyed my home to spend the best time I'd had left with my mom. I wear my ring to remind me never trust this way again. Oh there're so many reasons like the one I told you of. As fall leaves start to fall, and new colors arrive, maybe one will fall my way and I'll learn to trust again. But until that day comes, I'll wear my wedding rings to remind me <u>NEVER TRUST</u> that way again.

Love really can hurt sometimes . . . .

* *

<u>11/1/95 - 9 p.m.</u>
Still no call from Billy or his mom on the information I need for police.

Police called about 3 times asking if I got VIN numbers and plate numbers yet. They want me to call the Summary Section at 312-747-5533, Case #2515716 when I get the information for them or to let them know if Billy picked up car and van.

I'm beginning to think he must have; otherwise, I feel I would have heard something by now.

Well, every since my court date on Oct. 23, I haven't had any phone calls on Caller ID from people I don't know. Strange isn't it?

About 10:45 p.m. someone dropped that old pool table upside down in the back of the house. It woke me up. Sounded like the damn house was falling in. I had the alarm set on house. I just lay still in my bedroom. It only happened once, and it hasn't happened in a long time. They used to do it late at night 2 or 3 times. Well, if they were trying to scare the shit out of me, they did!

<u>11/2/95</u>
Police called 3 times.

<u>11/3/95</u>
Police called 1 time.

<u>Sun. 11/5/95</u>
Police called 9:30 a.m. to tell me they can't start looking for car and van without identification numbers or plate numbers. They asked me to inform my husband to go to any police station, bring titles with him, ask for Summary Section, and give police reports 2515716 (car) and 2515715 (van).

<u>11/6/95 - 8:30 a..m.</u>
Mailed letter to Attorney Starks' office about stolen car and van, since Billy didn't reply to message I sent him by my mother-in-law Oct. 31, 1995. I don't know what else to do but let my attorney know what's going on. It's funny Billy acted a fool when I moved the car and van from side of house to side of garage, and now I don't hear anything about them being stolen. Well, Lord, I've done all I can do. Maybe he towed them just to keep me all upset. (P.S. Also left message about this on attorney's fax machine.)

5:30 p.m. - No therapy today. Mrs. Watts' husband is dying from cancer. She's looking for him to pass any time. She looked so sad at our last group meeting. She said she would let us know when we will meet again. When I talked to her last Sunday, she said writing is just as good as talking. So I'll be writing in this little book when I'm upset . . . .

7:45 p.m. - I called my mother-in-law to see if Billy had left me a message. I reminded her I need ID numbers for van and car. She said when she told Billy what happened, all he said was I was responsible for everything he left here. Then with the next breath, my mother-in-law said, "Well, with the way things are, we don't have to exchange Xmas gifts this year. We can just send Xmas cards." We have been exchanging gifts since I moved in with her and Billy in Nov. 1982. This really hurt me, so I think this will be the last call or anything I have to do with her from now on.

11/13/95 - 7:45 a.m.
Mailed papers to Mr. Starks.

6:21 p.m. - I called the Summary Section (for stolen cars and vans, 312-747-8254) to see if Billy had turned in information to police station on car and van. The computer was slow, and the officer said he would call me back or for me to call back in 15 mins. to find out if the police reports were finished. Computer still down 7:09 p.m. Said try my call tomorrow.

Tues 11/14/95
Called 312-747-8254 at 7:56 a.m. Officer checked both police reports #2515716 and 2515715 and said they weren't put in the computer system yet. They're still waiting on information from Billy. Officer said, "Maybe your husband came and got it and just didn't tell you." Well, I've tried. As of today, I'm washing my hands of the damn car and van!

9:30 a.m. - Went to 10420 S. Halsted and signed up for Low Income Home Energy Assistance Program.

Haven't felt good. My back is killing me off and on.

11/16/95 - 5:30 p.m.
Two guys I had never seen before were standing outside in the vacant lot when I came in. As I got close to the house, they started walking toward me. As I turned to come up steps, they stopped at end of walkway facing me, talking loud about, "It's a shame men get put out of their homes and have to start over. Well, you know this man got put out (never saying a name), but he's buying a home in Country Club Hills or trying to now." By this time, I'm in the house walking fast, locked doors, and as I took my coat off, I looked out living rm window. They had moved to middle of the yard facing the window, talking even louder, saying the same thing as though if I hadn't hear them the 1st time, I would the 2nd time. I walked away from the window. They stood there for about 4 more minutes and then left. Had on hats and dark clothes. I stepped away from the window because my husband had already threatened

me that people died in drive and walk-by shootings everyday, and people never find their killers, so I'm always scared when stuff like this happens.

11/17/95

Well, hell! This morning my nerves were shot! Everything that moved I thought was following me. But what took the cake was this tall, thin man—blue cap, short jacket, blue jeans, dark—was standing with his arm folded in his jacket at the Washington-O'Hare "L" stop on the other side of me about 4 feet away, just staring at me. I moved, he'd move. Finally the lady next to me noticed and asked me if I knew him. I said no. I think if it wasn't my train that was coming at that moment, I'd caught the wrong one just to get away from him.

12/7/95

Well, I haven't slept at all these past few days, and I've taken sleeping pills the doctor gave me for about 4 nights. I know it's because I have to go to court and be around him, but I'm glad it's almost over. My nerves are shot. And it doesn't help any that I have to repeat everything a second time. April 14, 1994, I was in court from 9 a.m. to 5:21 p.m.

Everything I eat won't stay on my stomach, and to top that off, my little piece of part-time job may end Dec. 15 till after the new year. Every year I fix the house up so pretty with Xmas lights everywhere. This year, I'm just not in the Xmas mood. I'm sick of repeating everything over in court that went on with his 1st lawyer. You know, it's funny. Billy asked for a divorce Oct. 1993. I told him to go file; he never did. When I finally had enough, I did in June '94, and he has done everything to put it off by dragging me back and forth to court. I wonder why he thinks I'm going to change my mind about what I want in the divorce. Taking me back a 2nd time for a round-table meeting is only making me mad because I haven't changed my mind, and I have to pay my attorney money I don't have again to say so. Oh well, I'll take 2 more sleeping pills, and toss and turn all night, and just maybe, I'll really get a good night's sleep after Friday . . . and find my great wonderful Xmas mood as I normally have. I still get a lot of phone calls everyday between 9 a.m. and 4:30 p.m., but they won't leave a message on my answering machine. Oh well, it's their quarter—not mine.

12/8/95 - 12:10 p.m.

My attorney, Mr. Starks, called and said the court judge, Ms. Dickler, had canceled the court date; will reset another time and day. Mr. Starks received $100.00 I sent.

12/15/95

My back went out again. Was in bed and house till Dec. 29, 1995. Couldn't work or anything. Still getting crazy phone calls:

12/21/95
    1:20 p.m. - 312-375-9776 - Ernest Nazon

12/22/95
    3:50 p.m. - 312-568-3664 - Lue Bock

12/25/95
    10:54 a.m. - 312-667-4565 - C. B. Clark
    5:35 p.m. - 312-962-0358 - Brenda Sims

New Year - New Beginning for me - 1/1/96 - 9 a.m.
Called my sister and mother-in-law. They were doing great. I really enjoy talking with my mother-in-law.

1/6/96 - 7 a.m.
Somebody was in backyard. Billy's Mustang car door was open and also side gate on the house.

1/20/96
Tony came over about 1:45 p.m. to fix boiler in basement. It had been leaking 4 pails of water a day. Valve was broke. Went to Ace's on 111th St., got valve and flashlight. He only charged me $60.00 cash to fix it. The boiler man wanted $150.00. (Took pictures.)

1/21/96 - 9:36 a.m.
Somebody was in backyard last night about 1:17 a.m. banging on back door and back of house. When I went outside this morning, I had to shut side gate on house. They left it open again.

2/2/96
Brinks (1-800-445-0872) called 9:57 a.m. about my alarm going off. Neighbor (Ms. Queenie) called about 10:05 a.m. to see what was happening. Both left a message on my answering phone.

**Ms. Hill hasn't called since 10/95. 2:45 Belinda Hill called (312-264-4070).

2/3/96
Well, it is now 8:05 a.m. Sat. morning and I keep hearing this noise in basement. Finally, I get up to see what the hell is going on!

8:31 a.m. - There's a European baby Starling bird flying in hall of lower basement stairs. I don't know how scared he was, but he scared the shit out of me when I hit the top stairway! I took a few pictures after he settled down some.

Then opened back door and screen, and about 2 minutes later, he flew out. I don't know how he got in. All windows are closed. Well, let me call Brinks. My play dad was upset by Brinks when they called and he couldn't find me to tell them my story for today.

2/15/96
Talked with Billy's mom. She is OK. Talked with her best friend, Mrs. Otis. She's OK. Had to tell me that Billy and new girlfriend, Julia, and kids had been at Mom's for Xmas dinner. (Otherwise, you hardly see her and kids.)

2/17/96 - 4:20 p.m.
I ordered a pizza, but they didn't have delivery today, so I had to go pick the pizza up, which started a chain of events you wouldn't believe!

First, on return with the pizza, the front door lock slipped and I was locked out, so I went to the back door, broke the screen, wiggled and twisted till I opened screen door, and then broke glass to open main door. My neighbor looked out and smiled after she saw it was me and said I was a noisy crook. Finally, 15 minutes later I'm in. Now, I had to call someone to fix the mess I made, so I called Tony. He came over and patched everything up for now. Will fix totally later.

Well, I bought 2 new movies. First off, "Cliffhanger" didn't work. Got caught on the heads of VCR and I had to take VCR apart to get it out. So I watched the other movie, "What's Love Got to Do with It?," a true story of Tina Turner and Ike. Well, this movie reminded me of what Billy and I went through.

Well, hell! I had a nightmare. Somebody had broken in the upstairs and was living up there till one day they started fighting and tore the place up. Kids were crying and a woman was screaming. Now, my kitchen door to upstairs was locked, but this half-beaten baby cat and dog were walking across my kitchen. I flushed the cat down toilet; then I did the same to the dog, but his ear stopped him from going down. The harder I tried to get rid of him, the harder he fought to live. Finally, I woke up. Boy, I won't watch that movie no more!

2/18/96
It's quiet and I'll just bird watch and video the backyard today. Well, I saw red birds, Blue Jays, Finches, Nutchers, Black Cap Chickadees, Sparrows, Downy Woodpeckers, Mourning Doves, and European Starlings. It was a great day for bird watching. I have 32 feeders. I made a pond for them in summer and spring and planted about 1,000 flowers around here for them.

Can't wait till spring so I can see all my feathered summer birds return. They have been coming for 10 years, now. It's sad that this may be my last year with them. (5:10 p.m.)

2/23/96 - 6 a.m.
My back gate was open and Billy's Mustang car door was open. Trashcans were knocked over. I don't know if someone is sleeping back there or stealing parts. I called and left a message on my attorney's answering machine this morning (Sat.) to let him know what was happening.

2/24/96
11: 45 a.m. doctor's appt. New doctor at the clinic now. He wants me in back therapy. I have to call Monday to make arrangements. I don't think my back will ever get right after being kicked from dining room table Nov. '93. I hurt something in middle of my feet on sharp edge and that still hurts off and on. I guess it'll never heal.

My neighbor, Mr. Clayton, came over to check on me because I'm always walking and Ms. Miller across from me hadn't seen me, was worried, and mentioned it to him. I told him my back went out on me again and I was just staying in again for awhile but thanked them for worrying about me.

3/3/96 - 7:05 p.m.
Today was nice. My godmother surprised me with a birthday dinner. I had a nice time.

When I checked my Caller ID, I saw my neighbor, Mrs. Annie Baker, had called about 5 p.m., so I returned her call a few minutes ago. She was worried that I was sick again because she hadn't seen me in my backyard for awhile.

3/9/96 - 10:35 a.m.
I went to Jewel to pick up tokens and pictures from Osco (about 10:16 a.m.). I walked out of Jewel toward Popeyes Chicken. As I was crossing the street, 2 shots were fired as an off-white Rambler with no plates went right by me. As I looked back to see who it was, the little old man next to me pushed me across the street in front of him saying, "You don't stand still when someone is shooting at you." I said, "Are you sure? Maybe the car backfired." He said, "That was gun shots." Well, hell! I think I'll be in for the rest of the weekend. The whole time I remember Billy saying to me, "It's always a way to get rid of someone. Drive-by shootings happen all the time." All of that came back to me.

3/11/96 - 5:40 p.m.

I was outside talking with neighbors trying to see if any strange guys were around the house at any time driving an old off-white Rambler. They said no but I should report it to the police in case it happens again. My brother, Herby, is totally upset.

3/18/96

Started on new P.T. job with Kelly. Riding on busses and train took a lot out of me. Go back on Thursday for 4 hrs. and Friday. Can't miss any days or I'll be replaced. Lite filing and answering phone. I called Special Services with CTA to see if I could sign up to have van pick me up. Said it would take 5 to 7 days before I get form. Must have doctor sign it and send back in.

3/19/96

A.J. fixed arch on back doorway to keep squirrels and birds from coming in the house. Both sides of archway were rotted out. Put metal plate up.

Calls on Caller ID:

      2/6/96 - 5:28 p.m. - Derita Keller - 312-660-8747

      2/7/96 - 8:26 p.m. - Fannie Pollard - 312-762-6705

      2/14/96 - 5:33 a.m. - Stimsonsonite Corp - 708-647-7191

      2/17/96 - 12:33 p.m. - unavailable - 312-986-0597

      2/22/96 - 4 p.m. - Johnie MA - 312-434-2535

      3/9/96 - 9:42 a.m. - Padieu Hammond - 312-375-0226

      3/13/96 - 7:38 p.m. - unavailable - 312-271-9162

      3/14/96 - 8:24 p.m. - Deborah Todd - 708-489-6465

      3/15/96 - 3:33 p.m. - D. Griffin - 312-846-0363

      3/19/96 - 6:57 p.m. - Renee Ware - 847-486-1821

      3/20/96 - 1:43 p.m. - Home & Yard Improv. - 312-736-8669

      3/21/96 - 5:57 p.m. - Starks Associates - 312-995-7737

            6:42 p.m. - Charlene Ladner - 312-928-1052

            9:34 p.m. - anonymous Ameritech call. Someone reported trouble on my line.

            8:26 p.m. - Bert called. He went to hospital today.

            6:54 p.m. - Job called to see what was going on with message I left. (Sharon was away from desk. Talk to Peggy.)

3/21/96 - 5:40 p.m.

Well, I'm tired as hell. Long day. When I get home, I always check my answering service. Today only one call and it was from my attorney's office. Time: 4:57 p.m. (Call 16 on numbers I keep.) Then when I went in, I saw I had 1 new call on answering machine. It was my attorney's office, but the

IN THE CIRCUIT COURT OF COOK COUNTY, ILLINOIS

0000055.1666

In re the Marriage of
Deborah Harvey,
            Petitioner

96

v.

William Harvey, III,
            Respondent

NO. 94 D 4432
4363
4215
4363
4406

ENTERED

MAR 2 2 1996 (m)

GRACE G. DICKLER - 1521

ORDER

This matter coming to be heard on the Pre-trial conference call, all parties being present and represented by Counsel, and the Court being fully advised in the premises.

It is Hereby Ordered:

1) Petitioner must disclose all witness to Respondent within 14 days

2) Petitioner's medical records of all treating physicians must be tendered to Respondent within 21 days

3) The current Order of Protection which expires on April 14, 1996 is extended until the date of trial, over Respondents objection

4) This matter is continued to 4-16-96, 9:30 for a Rule 215 witness status

Atty No.
Name
Attorney for #30753
Address Watkins & Sawyer
City   Atty for Respondent
Telephone 20 E. Jackson #500
         Chicago, Ill
         (312) 987-1197

_____ , 19 ___

ENTER:

_____ 157

Judge   Judge's No.

AURELIA PUCINSKI, CLERK OF THE CIRCUIT COURT OF COOK COUNTY, ILLINOIS

Court File Copy   CCG-2-75M-05-23-95 (53420210)

IN THE CIRCUIT COURT OF COOK COUNTY, ILLINOIS

DEBORAH HARVEY

v.

WILLIAM HARVEY, III

DOB - 6-28-55

0000055.1667

Case No. 94D 4432
96

LEEDS NO. ....

[ ] Independent Petition
[ ] Criminal Proceeding
[ ] Domestic Relations
4563

ENTERED

MAR 2 2 1996 KM

GRACE G. DICKLER - 1521

ORDER

The Court Finds that

[X] A Ex Parte Order of Protection was issued on April 14, 1994

[ ] An Order of Protection was issued on April 14

THE COURT HAVING JURISDICTION OF THE SUBJECT MATTER, IT IS HEREBY ORDERED THAT:

[✓] 1. An extension of the Ex Parte Order of Protection is granted and is hereby extended to April 16, 19 96, at 9:30 A m.

[ ] 2. A hearing on the Ex Parte Order of Protection is set for ....m., on .... 19...., in Courtroom No. ....

[ ] 3. The Ex Parte Order of Protection is vacated.

[ ] 4. The Order of Protection previously issued is extended to ...., 19....

[ ] 5. A hearing on the Order of Protection is set for ....m., on ...., 19...., in Courtroom No. ....

[ ] 6. The Order of Protection is vacated.

[ ] 7. [ ] The Ex Parte Order of Protection is modified as follows

    [ ] The Order of Protection is modified as follows

_____

_____

_____

Name STACKS + Boyd
Attorney for DEBORAH HARVEY
Address 11528 SO. Halsted
City C 490
Telephone 312- 995-7960

Enter: _____ Judge _____ Judge's No.

Date: ....

AURELIA PUCINSKI, CLERK OF THE CIRCUIT COURT OF COOK COUNTY, ILLINOIS 4

strange thing is they said they called before. This is the 1st message I've gotten from them saying I had to be in court Friday—no time, no room number—for court or anything. Well, I guess I'll go to court and sit till I see someone. I'll go to the court where we were supposed to be last time.

You know I've been out of Stress Therapy since Nov. '95. Before this is over, I'll be in Body and Stress Therapy 5 days a week! I'm still in shock over the message on my answering machine. I'm beginning to think Billy has bought my lawyer to throw the case his way. Well, I'm tired, broke, and my mind and body have had more than one person can take these past 2 yrs. Well, it's 6:42 p.m. and my godmother, Charlene, called to tell me she picked up my mail from P.O. Box today. Nothing important came. I asked her if anyone called them and left a message for me and she said no. I have one hell of a headache right now (6:53 p.m.). When I'm this upset, I shouldn't try to write. I can't think straight.

Well, I called the job and talked to Peggy. They'll replace me, and if that person doesn't work out, they'll give me a call. I started crying. She said she hoped everything turns out and to have a nice weekend. How the "H" can I think about the weekend! I'm going to take another 800 mg pain pill and try to get some rest.

It is now 7:01 p.m. With Express Temp, this makes the 2nd job I've lost and with Kelly, I've lost 3 since this whole mess started. I don't know how much more I can take! It's got to end soon!

Ameritech called at 9:34 p.m. to see if my phones were working. I told them they were fine. I asked who reported my line was not working. She said she didn't know. It was the 20th call on Caller ID and it showed up as an anonymous call. I hit Star 69 to redial whoever called to make sure it was them that called and they said Ameritech when they answered phone. Somebody is playing games and don't want me to get any sleep tonight.

3/22/96 - 6:51 a.m.
I called Mr. Starks' office and left a message. I would be in the courthouse by 8:30 a.m. to check the board for time, room, and judge since they gave me no information. I recorded the message to their office behind their message they left me. All week long I've had dozens of calls on Caller ID, 2 messages on answering machine—1 Monday and 1 from them Thurs. and now my recording which makes 3.

Well, it's 7:12 a.m. I'm getting ready to leave about 7:30 a.m.

Well, it's 9:04 a.m. I'm here. Checked the board—11:30 a.m. court time, Room 2102, Judge Grace B. Dickler. Well, Mr. Starks showed up. Nobody could agree on anything, so now we will go to trial and the judge will decide. My Order of Protection will be extended to after my divorce. Paid $100.00, Ck. 1256.

* *

Mar. 1996 (POEM)
A black rose is rare and beautiful . . .
Please handle me with care.
I have so much love to give . . .
With each new bloom . . .
So let me grow in your life,
Not kill or beat me . . .
Feed me sunshine, love, and water . . .

* *

5/7/96 - Starks' Office
Call in morning. Secretary wanted list of witnesses. Took to her at 3:30 p.m. She said I had a court date May 9, 1996 at 9 a.m., Room 2102. I asked if I needed witnesses, and she said, "No."

5/9/96
This was a nightmare! I reached the courthouse this morning to find my attorney wasn't there; his partner, Attorney Boyd, was there. Several hours later, Attorney Starks finally showed up. I didn't go before Judge Grace Dickler because we missed that time. We went before Judge Liekien. Now I'm before a judge that doesn't know my case. My attorney B.E. Starks wasn't fighting for me, so I tried to tell the judge what was happening. Well, the judge was upset with me and told me to speak when asked to. By this time, I was getting sick—sweating, lightheaded, and could hardly speak. The judge was asking me what I wanted out of the house. I was trying to speak but couldn't. Then the judge handed me some tissues to wipe the sweat off of me; I tried to talk but it wouldn't come out right. Then my husband saw that I was having trouble, so he said, "I think she said stove, refrigerator, etc." I felt like I was going to faint. Attorney Starks stuck me in the back with his pen a couple of times. I was glad it was almost over. Then I asked the judge about my Order of Protection. He looked at both attorneys and in a loud voice said, "What Order of Protection"?

Then I hear Starks and Sawyer whispering, "this can go wrong," so they spoke up, and it was extended again. Well, I fired Attorney Starks and got

"Your wife got the house, but I did manage to get you custody of the mortgage payments."

Attorney Birndorf to handle my case. The next court date, my Ex-Attorney Starks sat on my husband's side saying he was protecting his interest in the case. That let me know right then my husband bought him out, and he didn't care about me. I thought if I fired him, he shouldn't have been in court at all. He didn't let me have witnesses or my medical records. They were out because of a 215 ruling where Attorney Starks misdiaried the matter in his diary. I never got to tell the judge my husband had the Board of Health going to pick me up at my job at Lawrence Hall Youth Center. Because he wasn't man enough to tell me he had a problem 8/89 or that he carried me on his taxes for 88-89 and 90 as a child, mixing my Social Security number up. Attorney B. E. Starks was fired May 31, 1996. Next court date is June 5, 1996 at 1:30 p.m., Room 1502 with new Attorney Theodore Birndorf.

**(Notes in big book. Lost everything.) Attorney Starks acted like he was bought off by other side. He said he wrote my case off as a loss. I owe him nothing.

1st Deal - There was nothing for my medical costs after this deal for $4,800.00. That was $480.00 a month for 10 mos. Started 10 days after judgment. Out in 30 days. No money up front to move on. I said, "No." My medical costs would eat that. What was I to live on after it was gone? Out by June 9, 1996.

IN THE CIRCUIT COURT OF COOK COUNTY, ILLINOIS BB000065.0087

96

Deborah Horvey

v.

William Horvey, III

NO. 94 D 4432

4229

ENTERED
APR 16 1996 KM
GRACE G. DICKLER-152.

ORDER

This cause coming to be heard on the Court's
Order for a Rule 215 witness status, Respondent being
Represented by counsel, neither Petitioner nor counsel
for Petitioner present, this Court being fully advised in
the premises

IT IS HEREBY ORDERED that Petitioner
is precluded from introducing at trial any evidence
regarding the medical condition of Petitioner based on
Petitioner's failure to comply with the terms of the
March 20, 1996 Order entered by this Court.

From Debby B. Harvey
I made copies of the
following pages
July 30, 1996 at the
daley center when I look in my

Atty No. 30753
Name Watkins and Sawyer
Attorney for Respondent/Counter-Petitioner
Address 20 E. Jackson Blvd., #500
City Chicago, Il 60604
Telephone (312) 987-1197

ENTER:
_____ 150

Judge   Judge's No.

*divorce files
I was never
given these
papers*

AURELIA PUCINSKI, CLERK OF THE CIRCUIT COURT OF COOK COUNTY, ILLINOIS

COURT FILE COPY

CCG-2-70M-11-15-95(53420246)

5/10/96
Canceled food stamp appt. New date May 17, 1996 at 9:15 a.m. Called clinic to explain about spasm pain that had been going on all week in my back. I
got worried when the pain caused me not to be able to talk. Tried to explain.
I thought I had about 4 or 5 short heart attacks or something. She laughed
and told me to take my medicine to see if it would clear up. I still made a doctor's appt. for next wk. Called Chgo. Bar Association (554-2000).

5/11/96 - 11:30 p.m.
My play granny, Leola Nelson, loaned me $500.00.

5/13/96 - 9:30 a.m.
I went to Clerk's Office, "Levoyd" at 28 North Clark, Chgo., IL 345-8330
to see if I could get transcript for Case 94-D-4432 for these dates:
>   April 14, 1994 - Judge Phillip Bronstein
>   Mar. 22, 1996 - Judge Grace G. Dickler
>   May 9, 1996 - I realized I didn't know the judge's name, so Mr.
Levoyd took the other order and gave me Court Rep. to call at 443-5262 to
get judge's name. I tried a few times from there, but the line was busy. So Mr.
Levoyd said to try when I got home and call him back to place order for this
one. It will take about 2 to 6 wks. I said, "OK."

12:15 p.m. - I tried and tried. Line was busy. Finally, I got through to Court
Rep. 443-5262 and gave them the room and date. They couldn't find it. So I
said to try the 1st court room I was in— Rm 2102, 9 a.m., Judge Grace
Dickler. And it came up transferred to Judge Mitchell Liekien, Clerk
Number 443-500. So I called this number. Boy, was I surprised! It was the
judge. Now I'm scared, so I didn't say my name. (Judge Liekien was upset
with me in court May 9, 1996.) I said, "Judge Liekien, I was in court with you
May 9, 1996, Rm 1502, at 1:15 p.m. How do I get that transcript of court?"
He paused a few seconds and said, "Call the Clerk's Office and give room
number and the date." I said, "Thank you" and hung up. I would loved to
have had a penny for his thoughts right then. I called Mr. Levoyd back at
345-8330, and he couldn't find it, and his boss couldn't find it. So I gave up
on that for now . . . .

5/14/96
I called everywhere telling my story. Nobody could help. Chgo. Legal Clinic
(312-731-1762) gave me a few numbers. I called and left a message. Nobody
called yet. Well, I've received this request for investigation of a lawyer that
the Chgo. Bar Association said they would send. The lady I talked to said this
didn't sound right and I should fill it out. Well, I just did. Need to make some
copies of other things to send. I'll mail them a copy and have my main one

typed for Walter Jacobson (TV news anchor man) when I send him draft letter 3 of "My Last Tears" which is 9 pages. He has draft 2 of about 6 pages. I mailed it last Sat. (11th of May 1996). I know he'll never run across my letter with all the mail he gets. I'm scared and if anything happens to me, I want my story told of "My Last Tears."

Well, I'm back in the phone book and for some reason, I'm on the page with Theodore Birndorf's number looking at me. Maybe this is a sign from God that my prayers have been heard. So I called and he was in. Only heard a little of my story, took my number, and said he'd call me back. Well, I left to try to get some money and look at apts., and I missed the call, but he left a message. He tried to pull something up about the case, but it was listed under Billy's codes. Asked me to call his office by 7 p.m. or tomorrow to make an appointment to see him Wed., May 15, 1996 at 33 N. LaSalle, Rm 2500, 312-726-7331, and to bring all my papers.

Well, it's about 7:45 p.m., so I'm throwing stuff and looking everywhere for my divorce papers. I got a copy when Attorney Starks filed July 7, 1994 and I signed the paperwork on what I wanted in my divorce. Now I'm mad! Somebody had stolen this whole section when I was in court May 9, 1996, Rm 1502 in the little conference room. I had my paper then, and I haven't touched this bag until now. Now, I know I'm up shit's creek in a canoe going down stream, upside down, and damn! I can't swim!

It don't look like I'm ever going to stop crying my last tears. What am I going to tell Attorney Birndorf? I went all through this book, and I always keep everything in a section marked by a small label—that pink label and paper are all gone. My heart is beating so fast. I feel like I'm having a heart attack or something. All the dumb countersuit I went through and papers gone. So I remembered this Daily Diary I keep and wrote down as much as I could for him in notes of dates some things went on. That's the best I can do.

<u>5/15/96 - 9 a.m.</u>
I called and made appt. for 7:30 p.m. and off Charlene and sister Helen and I go downtown. I told my story and cried, and for some reason, my angel was with me once again. Attorney Birndorf would see what he could do. I was sorry due to the loss of my other papers. The rest of my notes will remain in my heart and mind . . . For I was told, "If your heart and mind are pure, that's the best note pad you need." My grandmom was Indian. They believed in things like that, and I loved to hear her talk, for most of the old sayings I heard have a lot of truth in them. Gave the attorney $500.00 I borrowed from Leola Nelson (312-277-7525).

11:15 a.m. - Attorney Starks' office called. His secretary, Enedra, said my judgment came and I could sign it. I said, "Not today—maybe tomorrow . . ."

5/16/96
Wrote all day. My godfather came over 10:45 a.m. He said he was worried about me and couldn't sleep. He just had to see me. He drove from Brookfield. We had lunch at Long John Silver's on 111th & Halsted. This was a nice surprise.

5/17/96 - 8:05 a.m.
Left home to Food Stamp appt. at 9:15 a.m. I arrived at 11203 South Ellis about 8:55 a.m. I signed up and the lady said, "You're early; I may get you early." Before I could sit down, my name was called. Everything was fine till they asked for something they could copy about my divorce. Well, I looked at Mr. Maisonet (660-7043) and said, "I don't have anything. Someone stole that from me, but I know somebody I can get you a letter from." He looked at me strange and gave me till the 28th of May to bring it in. I said, "Thanks."

PART III - A Ray of Hope

5/17/96 - 9:40 a.m.

I'm waiting for the bus, standing in a bus shelter, and this nice young man said, "Hello." I said, "Hi." He was talking about how hot it was. I said, "I know; I've got on too much myself." Then He asked what church I belonged to. I said none really since I left Charleston, W. VA at 19 yrs old. By now, another person, a lady by the name of Mary, walked up. I remember her name. She had beautiful gray eyes. So the young man told me about his church and that they have different programs. Now, most of the time, I'm a shy person, but this young man was determined I was going to talk. I said, "You know, you don't have to go to church to be a saved person."

I was in church every Sunday and Sunday School with my family, and I realized a long time ago as a child, it didn't matter whose church you went to— big or small, they had some of the biggest devils of all—starting with some preachers! Then he said, "All these Christians are fighting about who's right about the Word of God." I replied, "You know, as far as I know, God could be the color of a rainbow. I don't really know, but when you have a pure heart and mind, that's when you can feel your soul inside." Then I said, "I have chills all over." The lady said, "Amen."

"You like going to church—me, I'd rather help someone in need, which I've done all my life. My mother used to say my heart would be the death of me one day because I give it 100% and some. You know, it doesn't matter your color— blue, green, pink—when you die and you're under six feet of dirt, no one will know. They only see a name as they walk by. But for some reason, we all have red blood; we can exchange eyes, lungs, hearts, etc.; so He did make us as one . . . But if you have never felt your soul inside, now that's time to worry."

The little lady said, "Amen."

I said, "For some reason, you're trying to get me to your church. Don't worry, if not this Sunday. I watched your church one day on Channel 26 at 8 a.m. I've watched others preach on the bus, trains, and by-ways, but this is a first for me. The little lady said, "Amen."

"For as we stand here under this bus shelter, I've preached my best and only service. I've seen the light, and it's beautiful. I saw it before my sister died; I've felt the Spirit when my granddad and my father died. They both told me goodbye in a way that warmed my heart inside. As I was on my way from Chicago to Charleston, W. VA. trying to see them before they passed, I knew in my heart the minute they passed, for the warmth of them passed right through me. So, you see, I know I have a soul because I can feel it from time-to-time."

"Remember this always: The Indians, Spanish, French, and Americans all speak differently, but when they pray, we all pray to <u>One</u>. For when all our souls leave this body which is our home, we all will answer to only One in the end. So you see, we just had church in this little bus shelter, and there's more love here than in those big churches over there."

REMEMBERING "BACK IN THE DAY"

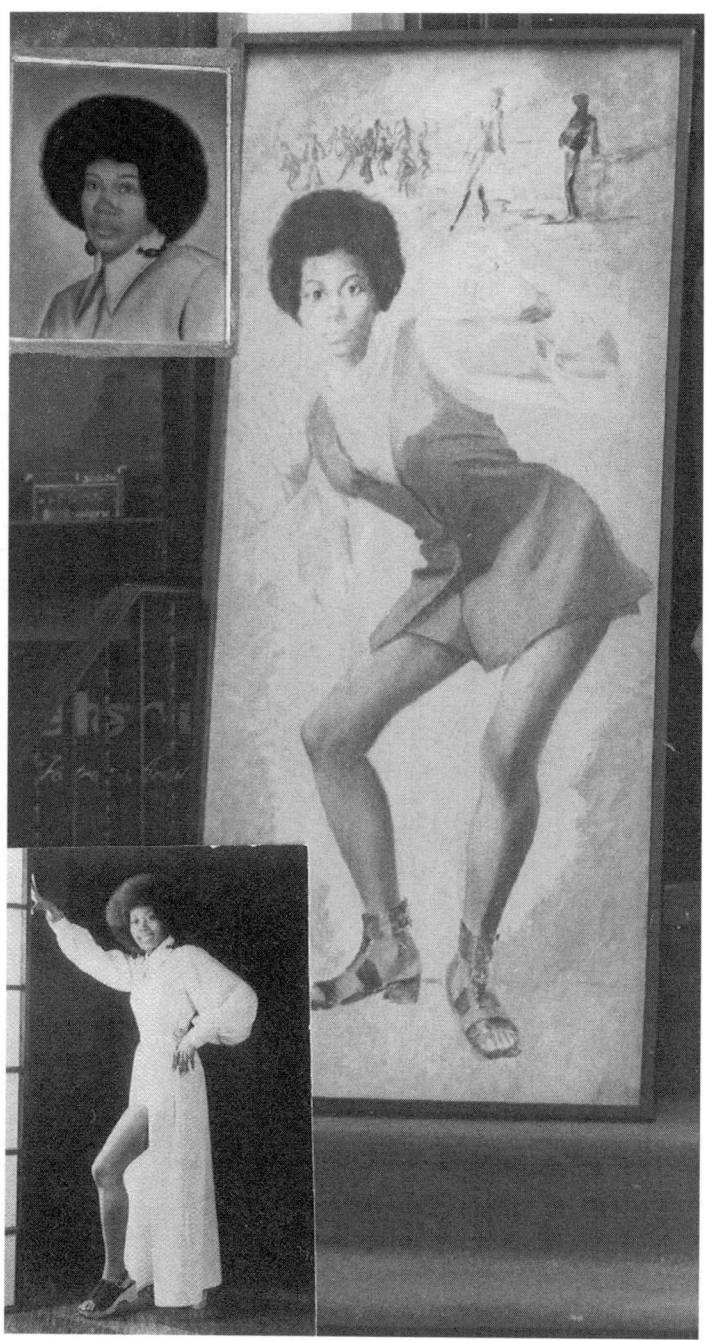

Then the young man said, "We have Bible Study." I said, "You don't need me, for now that I've started preaching, I may not stop." We all laughed. By now, the bus is here. The 3 of us still talk like we all are old friends. He got off at King Drive. As I got off at Halsted, I turned to Mary and said, "Bye. Have a nice day. But I want you to remember a book I want to write, *My Last Tears*." Everyone on the bus went totally quiet as I got off.

This was the best day I've had in a long time. Then an old girl friend called me, and we laughed and cried some about what I had been through. Anita and I both needed that long talk we had. This has really been a great day. (3:15 p.m.)

5/18/96 - 11:29 a.m.
Coordinated Adv. Legal Service (738-9486 or 738-9432) called returning call from last wk.

5/19/96
I saw my 1st Scarlet Tanager bird today in the middle of Bulls game. I got excited. Everyone thought I had lost my mind. Then they laughed. Everyone came over to watch the Bulls play. They won. They bought everything needed to cook out—food, beer, snacks. They all cheered me up a lot today.

5/20/96 - 3:58 p.m.
Attorney Birndorf's office called. I need to go in and sign new papers to over-turn what Starks and Sawyer did May 9, 1996 court date. Call Celia Ladner to go with me Tues. May 21, 96 at 10 a.m. Don't want to catch bus down-town by myself. Told Celia to meet me at 8:30 a.m. tomorrow.

5/21/96
Celia and I arrived at Attorney Theodore Birndorf's office at 9:30 a.m. for me to sign papers on notice of new motion.

5/22/96 - 9 a.m.
Took Food Stamp Office rest of papers they needed. Called Levoyd at Clerk's Office (345-8330, 28 N. Clark) about transcript from court May 9, 1996, Rm 1502. They still don't have anything. Said one of attorneys could have had a free-lance court Rm reporter.

4 p.m. - Doctor's apptment. Change blood pressure medicine 50 mg to 100 mg. Gave me new doctor's statement for CTA Disability pass and RTA services.

5/23/96 - 9:15 a.m.
I called Sharon 664-7200 Ext. 4581 to check on maintenance check from CTA. She said last check was issued 5/1/96, Check No. 726258, and I need to call Ms. Jerry Spencer 664-7200, Ext. 4534 to see why and when it was

stopped. She wasn't in yet, so I left a message for her. Then I called Attorney Birndorf and told him the check was issued, mailed him new medication list and doctor's statement, and also said I was worried my ins. and dental may be stopped.

10:38 a.m. - Talked to Ms. Spencer again. She called to say the delete order had to have been placed between 4/20/96 and 5/4/96 for me not to have gotten it.

2:38 p.m. - I called her back. Ms. Spencer tried but hadn't got the delete order date yet. She thinks it may be in Law Building. Didn't have time to go to that building yet. But she said she would call back.

<u>5/24/96</u>
Attorney Birndorf called about court date maybe next wk.

<u>5/27/96</u>
Received court date in mail—5/31/96.

<u>5/30/96</u>
Attorney Birndorf called to remind me about 9 a.m. court date 5/31/96. Called back later to say date was changed to 10:30 a.m.

<u>5/31/96</u>
Celia and I went to court. My ex attorney Starks, his asst., Mr. Boyd, Billy, and his attorney, Sawyer, were there. It really looked bad. Can't overturn what happened May 9, '96. Mr. Starks signed off as not being my attorney anymore. Whatever my old attorney did and said really didn't matter. Billy's attorney did everything by the book. My new attorney, Birndorf, really tried hard for me. Did get more money—$6,000.00 and $1,200.00 for me to move on. Did say if my doctors would come in to testify about my medical problem, may have a chance. I left court with some hope. New court day 6/5/96 at 1:30 p.m.

2nd Deal - New attorney much better, but they realize the 1st deal was rotten, so $1,200.00 to move. $6,000.00 is sum of $200.00 monthly pymts. No medical needs. Now I can move. What's $200.00 a mo. if I can end? I'll fight to win back my medical rights, to have a new attorney fight for permanent maintenance or alimony for the rest of my life, and for damages he caused. So be it! Maybe this way—somehow—I hope the whole thing can be thrown out and I can start again. I need COBRA Ins. or something. I can't live off of those other deals. If my back, inner ear, or blood pressure take a turn for the worse than now, what will I have? Nothing 5 or 10 yrs. from now!

THEODORE BIRNDORF
Attorney at Law

Suite 2500
33 North LaSalle Street
Chicago, Illinois 60602-2605
(312) 726-7331
FAX: (312) 641-3031

May 24, 1996

Honorable Judge Mitchell Leiken
Room 1502
Richard J. Daley Center
Chicago, Illinois 60602

Re: The Marriage of Deborah Brisco Harvey vs. William Harvey, III,
    Case No. 94 D 4432, Calendar C.

Dear Judge Leiken:

Enclosed are two motions that have been set for hearing May 31, 1996. I am forwarding them to you as courtesy copies.

Very truly yours,

Theodore Birndorf
/md (judge.ltr)

cc: Benjamin Starks
     Roderick T. Sawyer
     Deborah Harvey

Encs.

9 A.m. change 10/A.m.

IN THE CIRCUIT COURT OF COOK COUNTY, ILLINOIS
COUNTY DEPARTMENT - DIVORCE DIVISION

In Re: The Marriage of
Deborah Brisco Harvey,

No. 94 D 4432

                    Petitioner,
      Counter Respondent | Calendar 31

      and

William Harvey, III,

                    Respondent.
      Counter Petitioner

NOTICE OF MOTION

To: Roderick T. Sawyer
       Attorney at Law
       Law Office of Watkins and Sawyer
       20 East Jackson Boulevard
       5th Floor
       Chicago, Illinois 60604

       On   1996 at 9:30 a.m., or as soon thereafter as counsel may be heard, I
shall appear before the Honorable **Mitchell Leiken**, or any judge sitting in his stead, in the
courtroom usually occupied by him in **1502** at the Richard J. Daley Center, Chicago, Illinois, and
present the attached **Motion to Cancel Prove-up.**

Theodore Birndorf
Attorney for Petitioner/Counter Respondent
33 North LaSalle Street
Suite 2500
Chicago, Illinois 60602-2605
(312) 726-7331
Fax: (312) 641-3031
01187

CERTIFICATE AND AFFIDAVIT OF DELIVERY (PERSONALLY OR BY MAIL)

       The undersigned hereby certifies under penalties of perjury as provided by law pursuant
to Ill. Rev. Stat. Ch. 110, par. 1-109, that the above notice and any attached pleadings were [ ]
transmitted via fax from the Law Office of Theodore Birndorf, Phone Number: 312/641-3031 at
to above attorney at [ ] personally delivered or [X] placed in the U.S. Mail properly addressed,
with first class postage prepaid, to the parties at the addresses set forth above on or before
May 21, 1996 at 5:00 p.m.

                                        Theodore Birndorf
       Signature   (Print Name)

IN THE CIRCUIT COURT OF COOK COUNTY, ILLINOIS
COUNTY DEPARTMENT - DIVORCE DIVISION

In Re: The Marriage of
Deborah Brisco Harvey,

Petitioner,
Counter Respondent

and

William Harvey, III,

Respondent.
Counter Petitioner

No. 94 D 4432

Calendar 31

MOTION TO CANCEL PROVE-UP

NOW COMES the petitioner Deborah Harvey through her attorney Theodore Birndorf and says as follows:

1. She obtained a order of protection in June of 1994.

2. The respondent's Motion to Vacate the same was denied on June 28, 1994, the same order requiring respondent to remove certain items of personality from the marital premises.

3. The incident that was the subject of the Order of Protection occurred on November 27, 1993.

4. On that date respondent came home drunk and without cause, reason or provocation, while petitioner was speaking with respondent's mother on the telephone, put his hands around petitioner's neck, choked her, knocked the phone to the floor, knocked the chair to the floor, and notwithstanding that she had recent outpatient surgery for a cyst on the outside of her vagina, which had been lanced two days prior, respondent bruised her incision, pushed her down against the chair, which was on the floor sideways, with petitioner's back pressed against the metal side of the chair, and respondent jumped on top of her, grinding the lower part of her back into the chair, and knocking her head onto the floor at which time he continued to beat her causing her to lose consciousness several times. Respondent thereupon wrapped the telephone cord around her neck, destroyed the telephone and as soon as petitioner was able to, she left the marital home.

5. Benjamin Starks continued to represent her in the divorce case.

6. She has recently learned that on March 22, 1996 the court ordered the parties to furnish their witness list within two weeks and their medical records within three weeks, and continued the Order of Protection to the time of trial.

7. On May 7, 1996 her attorney's secretary telephoned her and asked her to bring in a list of witnesses for the prospective trial.

8. Petitioner brought in a list of witnesses to her attorney the same day, the seventeen witnesses contained on the list having previously agreed to testify for petitioner when the matter proceeded to trial. A copy of her witness list is attached hereto as Exhibit "A".

9. When petitioner brought her witness list into her attorney's office her attorney's secretary told her that she should appear in court at 9:00 a.m. on May 9, 1996 to obtain a trial date.

10. Her attorney's secretary told her at that time that she did not need her witnesses in court on May 9, 1996 as the May 9th date was only to obtain a future trial date.

11. When petitioner appeared in court on May 9th her medical problems were causing her substantial distress.

12. Her medical problems consist primarily of her bruised lower back caused by the trauma incurred by respondent on November 27, 1993 the facts of which are more fully described in paragraph 4. of this motion.

13. The doctor's diagnosis with regard to that injury was a bruise to the lower back, and the prognosis was that it would not improve, and probably would get worse over the years.

14. The doctor forbade her to do any heavy lifting and to refrain from strenuous activities.

15. In addition to the back injury, when respondent knocked petitioner's head against the floor on November 27, 1993, she began to have inner ear problems causing dizziness especially with head movements or ambulation.

16. Her doctor's directions to her included bed rest for two weeks each time she had dizzy spells.

17. In addition thereto, the hypertension suffered by petitioner has been exacerbated by the beating and the stress of this divorce, and her blood pressure often elevates to the point where it can cause a stroke.

18. When petitioner arrived in court on May 9, 1996 prior to 9:00 a.m. her attorney was not there, but respondent's attorney and respondent's mother were there.

19. Petitioner's attorney arrived about 9:20 a.m., but prior to that time his associate, Mr. Boyd, told petitioner that they would have to go to room 1502. When petitioner asked him whether she would need witnesses, noting the presence of respondent's mother, she was told that she would not need witnesses at that time.

4

20. Petitioner's attorney arrived about 9:20 a.m. in room 1502 and told petitioner that she would have to decide what she was going to do. Petitioner responded that she wanted to go to trial, not realizing that the matter had been assigned for trial.

21. Petitioner's attorney told her that if the matter went to trial the house would have to be sold, and because there was a minus equity, she would have to pay forty-percent of the deficiency, and that the only other alternative would be to refinance the house but that she could not do so because she was unemployed.

22. When petitioner asked her attorney why she would have to refinance the house he would not answer her.

23. Petitioner stated that she probably could keep the house if she continued to receive the alimony payments, but her attorney told her at that time that the courts don't give more than six months alimony in Illinois any more.

24. He then told her that respondent would pay her $4800.00 and retain the house if she would come to an agreement.

25. Petitioner stated that she would consider the same but would have to remain on his medical insurance because of her back spasms, her ear problems and hypertension continued to require medical treatment. Petitioner's attorney would not respond to that request, and told her only that her only choice was to accept $4800.00 from her husband, give him the house, and she would have to move within thirty days.

26. She asked if there was any alternative, such as trial, and her attorney told her that there was no alternative and she accepted the same.

27. By the time petitioner left the conference room to the court petitioner's blood pressure had increased to the point where she could barely speak, and when she was able to get out words, they were slurred and unintelligible. Her husband had to attempt to translate her answers to the court.

28. In the meantime, respondent withdrew the $4800.00 offer and agreed only to pay her $480.00 monthly for ten months starting in thirty days. When petitioner asked that it be paid by withholding order, her attorney told her that such payments could not be the subject of a withholding order.

29. During the hearing, petitioner's attorney would not let her speak of her medical problems, and made no mention of the order of protection. When she mentioned the order of protection, the judge stated he did not know anything about an order of protection because no one had advised him of the same.

30. At the time of the hearing, petitioner was dizzy and in substantial pain, and was unable to concentrate.

31. At the same time, her attorney gave her false advice.

32. On May 9, 1996, petitioner was unprepared for trial because her attorney had told her that the matter will not proceed to trial that day, but only that a trial date would be established that day, and she therefore did not have her witnesses in court. Her attorney had made no attempt to prepare her for the hearing.

33. The erroneous information given to her by her attorney combined with the debitated physical condition of petitioner put her in a position where she was not able to comprehend what was happening, or to make intelligent decisions.

34. She is unable to financially support herself, and has been unable to financially support herself since her husband traumatized her physically and emotionally on November 27, 1993.

35. In addition thereto, the medication that petitioner was taking pursuant to prescription at that time consisting of fifty milligrams of tenormin, twenty-five milligrams of elovial, and fifty milligrams of atenolol, which caused her to be in a state of confusion and unable to concentrate or make proper decisions.

36. By the time the hearing ended, petitioner was so dizzy she could barely stand, and was afraid of passing out, and was substantially unaware of what was going on in the court room.

37. Petitioner is without funds to pay her attorney.

WHEREFORE petitioner prays as follows:

A. That the results of the hearing of May 9, 1996 be cancelled.

B. That this matter be reset for hearing.

C. That petitioner be granted leave to conduct discovery.

D. That respondent be required to pay petitioner's attorney's

fees.

E. For such other relief as the court may grant to petitioner.

Deborah Harvey

CERTIFICATION

Under penalties as provided by law pursuant to Section 1-109 of the Code of Civil Procedure, the undersigned certifies that the statements set forth in this instrument are true and correct, except as to matters therein stated to be on information and belief and as to such matters the undersigned certifies as aforesaid that she verily believes the same to be true.

Deborah Harvey

THEODORE BIRNDORF
Attorney for Petitioner
33 North LaSalle Street
Suite 2500
Chicago, IL 60602-2605
(312) 726-7331
FAX: (312) 641-3031
1187

IN THE CIRCUIT COURT OF COOK COUNTY, ILLINOIS

In Re: The Marriage Of:

Deborah Brisco-Harvey
         Petitioner
         v.Counter-Respondent

William Harvey, III
         Respondent.
         Counter-Petitioner

NO. 94 D 4432

ORDER

This cause coming to be heard on Petitioner, Counter-Respondent's Motion to Cancel Prove-up - hereafter referred to as a Motion to Re-open Prove up - both parties being present and represented by counsel, Attorney for Respondent, Counter-Petitioner tendering a Judgment for Dissolution of Marriage in open court, the Court being advised in the premises.

IT IS HEREBY ORDERED that both Petitioner's Motion to Re-open prove-up and Respondent's request for an Entry of Judgment be entered and continued to June 5, 1996 at 1:30 PM in Room 1502.

Atty No. 30753
Name Watkins + Sawyer
Attorney for Respondent
Address 20 E. Jackson Blvd. #500
City Chicago Il 60604
Telephone (312)987-1197

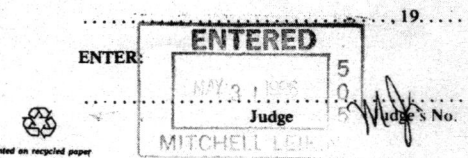

ENTER:

ENTERED
MAY 3 1996
Judge
MITCHELL LEIB

19.....

Judge's No.

AURELIA PUCINSKI, CLERK OF THE CIRCUIT COURT OF COOK COUNTY, ILLINOIS

ORDER   CCG-2

IN THE CIRCUIT COURT OF COOK COUNTY, ILLINOIS

IN RE': THE MARRIAGE OF

DeBorah Brisco Harley,
        Petitioner
        Counter Resp.

                And v.   NO. 94 D 4432

                                             Enc. 31

William Harvey, III,
        Respondent
        Counter Pet.   **ORDER**

This matter having come before The Court on The Motion of Deborah Brisco Harvey To discharge her Attorney of Record Benjamin E. Starks, Alleging Loss of Confidence The Court having heard The Request in Open Court and Said Attorney Benjamin E. Starks having no Objection The Court hereby ORDERS:

That Said Attorney Benjamin E. Starks is discharge instanter As The Attorney of Record for Deborah Brisco Harvey. Leave is given To Attorney Theodore Barndouf To file his Appearance instanter.

Atty No. 23771
Name STarks and Boyl
Attorney for Deborah Harley.
Address 1528 So. Halsted St.
City Chicago
Telephone 312-995-7900

ENTER: ...., 19.96.

ENTERED

MAY 3 1996

Judge MITCHELL LEIKIN Judge's No.

50.5

#28823

IN THE CIRCUIT COURT OF COOK COUNTY, ILLINOIS
COUNTY DEPARTMENT, DOMESTIC RELATIONS DIVISION

DEBORAH HARVEY)
    Plaintiff,)
)
)
v.) NO . 94 D 4432
)
)
WILLIAM HARVEY, II)
    Defendant.)

NOTICE OF MOTION

TO:

    WATKINS & SAWYER
    ATTN.: Mr. Roderick T. Sawyer
    20 E. Jackson Boulevard, Fifth Floor
    Chicago, IL 60604

You are hereby notified that on the 26th day of April, 1996 at 9:30 a.m. I will appear before the Honorable Judge sitting in room 2102 of the Daley Center and present the enclosed Motion to Reconsider.

ATTORNEY CERTIFICATE OF SERVICE

I, Benjamin E. Starks, an attorney in Illinois, hereby state that I served a copy of the above notice on individuals named above by placing the same in a sealed, addressed and stamped envelope and deposited the same in a US mail box on the 23rd day of April, 1996, and **via facsimile.**

                                       Benjamin E. Starks

Starks & Boyd, P.C #28823 11528 S. Halsted Chicago, IL 60628   312-995-7900

IN THE CIRCUIT COURT OF COOK COUNTY, ILLINOIS

IN RE THE MARRIAGE OF
DEBORAH B. HARVEY,
Pett.

0000079.0799

96

v.

NO. 94D 4432

WILLIAM HARVEY, III,
Resp.

5246

ENTERED
APR 2 6 1996   KM

GRACE G. DICKLER - 1521

ORDER

This matter having come before The Court
Re: An Order entered April 16, 1994, Precluding
The Petitioner from introducing Medical evidence
at Trial. The Court having been Advised
herein And Orders: The Motion to
Reconsider is denied

Atty No. 2-3721
Name   STARKS + Boyd
Attorney for   Petitioner
Address   11528 So. Halsted St.
City   CH90
Telephone   312-995-7900

_____ , 19____

ENTER:

_____
Judge   Judge's No.

AURELIA PUCINSKI, CLERK OF THE CIRCUIT COURT OF COOK COUNTY, ILLINOIS

COURT FILE COPY

CCG-2-70M-11-15-95(53420246)

You know, I really believed Mr. Starks was fighting for what I wanted. Due to medical problems my husband caused, I would remain in my home with alimony or something for the rest of my life. Boy, did he sell me out! Now for the next 3 mos., I have to live with nothing, hoping my doctor will testify to what's in my records to undo the mess Mr. Starks has me in . . .

Attorney Birndorf wanted me to get a note from CTA about when maintenance check was stopped; so Celia and I headed to the Merchandise Mart Building to CTA Payroll, 7th floor; asked to speak to Ms. Spencer. We were told she just left but to go to Rm 714. Someone would help us. Mr. Brown, who was Ms. Spencer's supervisor, listened to my story and read my notes where I had talked to Ms. Spencer. Then he looked for papers I needed copies of. Well, hell! He looked and had someone else to look. They found it but couldn't find original delete orders. What they found was that it was deleted between 4/20/96 and 5/4/96 on the printout he had, but the date it was deleted wasn't there. So he took my name and attorney's name and number with fax number and said he would keep looking. I said I needed it as soon as possible. He gave me his number 664-7200, Ext. 4531. I said, "Thanks" and left.

Next stop Dr. Office for medical records and to see if my doctor would testify for me. Well, he was in. Nurse Jean wrote me a letter and copied all my medical records for me. I thanked her, and Celia and I went home.

Well, I checked my messages and Mary Ann had called, and she said she didn't have a transcript for Mar. 22 but she was in the court Rm 2102. She said check my dates and place order again. I will Monday.

4:53 p.m. - Attorney Birndorf called; wanted my doctor's number so he could call him. I gave it to him.

6 p.m. - My play granny came by to see me and gave me money to grocery shop with.

9:41 p.m. - Somebody has been calling and hanging up on me all evening. "Unavailable" shows on Caller ID. I finally put my answering machine on to screen calls. When they hear that, they just hang up.

6/1/96 - 2 p.m.
For some strange reason, I felt sad all day. Then I took a walk to heaven, which was my attic. I started looking and looking, really not finding anything I wanted. Then something started my feet to the back of the attic. Went thru 2 boxes and I found old bank books, so I just kept looking and I started

singing "God Loves Me" because all morning I was trying to figure out what I had done that He would just forget about me down here. But I guess He had to let me know in His own way He had me in the palm of His hands all along because when I saw this old folder with 3 sides, I just started singing "I'm oh so happy—God does love me," for I found all the old bank statements I needed for court Wed. 5/5/96 at 1:30 p.m., Rm 1502!

You know, I've been all alone for the past 2 weeks. When you have a pure heart and mind, God always shows you the way to go when the time is right. You know, I always thought I couldn't have children, but when the time is right, I will. I've been dreaming about twins off-and-on. I just know one day soon I'll have my hands full, and I'll be saying, "How did Mom make it with 6 of us?" But she did, and if I give mine 1/2 that love she gave us, I'll be all right when that time comes too. Thank God for being there for me today and always. (4 p.m.)

6/4/96 - 5:44 a.m.
Having almost same attack like May 9—dizzy, lightheaded, vision shot, and lost voice. Pain everywhere in my back. I was hot and cold May 9, but this time, the pain was in right ear. I lay in bed unable to move for about a minute or 2—my face tightening up like your feet when they go to sleep. This happened twice. I finally got myself together and took blood pressure pills. I tried to make a phone call. Whether I did or not, I don't know. I remember lying back down. Now this is what really scared the hell out of me. I woke up about 7:01 a.m. vision still off and that tingling feeling in face. I was looking for my blood pressure machine but noticed I had unplugged clock in the bedRm, so I looked at clock on the wall over bed after I found my glasses. Then I realized all the lights were on in house and my refrigerator was turned off. What the hell did I do between 5:44 a.m. and 7 a.m.!

Blood Pressure Readings:
        7:10 - 141/128 Pul 65
        7:22 - 124/100 Pul 63
        8:24 - 131/96 Pul 61
        9 a.m. - 142/97 Pul 62 (My vision is still off some.)
            152/94 Pul 58. Called Vital Clinic 9:31 a.m. Talked with Cynthia. I read my blood pressure readings. She made me a 4 p.m. appointment.
        2:38 p.m. - Vision still off. I'm going to make appointment to see eye doctor if Billy hasn't taken his insurance from me.
        4:45 p.m. - 150/100

<u>6/5/96</u>

I asked Celia, "Did I call them yesterday morning early?" She said, "No." I talked to somebody that morning. I told her what happened.

<u>6/7/96</u>

Well, I started packing today. Billy is supposed to give me $480.00 to move today. The storage co. closes at 6 p.m. I knew in my heart he was going to act right. Well, he finally called my godmother and said he would bring the money to her for me about 10 p.m. Now, I've got to be out of the house by 6/9/96. Everyone I had planned on to help me tonight can't move me now, so I borrowed $100.00 to at least get the storage area from my godfather, and he brought me a lot of moving boxes. At least my godsister and a friend could start packing some things. Well, he finally brought the money about 10 p.m. I didn't have manpower or a truck, so what am I'm supposed to do? About 5:23 p.m. I had called my attorney to let him know, and he said because he was late, I could have one more day. So now I have Sunday also to move.

<u>6/8/96</u>

Well, they turned the gas off. So now I take this check to his bank, which was crowded as hell, and stood in line forever it seems. Finally, I reach the window. Teller 15 was a nice young man. First of all, the check was in my maiden name. I go by Harvey, so I had to sign the check twice, and they took forever to OK this check. They asked for everything but my shoe size. Finally now, I'm OK, I guess. They cashed the check and gave me $479.00 and charged me a $1.00 fee. I say "No, I can't take this. It must be $480.00, nothing less." Well, they explained I had to pay a fee. After 10 mins., I said. "Fine, but I need a receipt to show the court." (He still didn't mean well about the deal.) So now we go around and round about the receipt for a dollar. So I said, "Fine. I'll take you to court about my $1.00." The supervisor said, "Miss, you would spend $20.00 to go through court for $1.00?" And I said, "Yes. The deal was I get $480.00 to move on from my home of 12 yrs, and nothing else. My husband got the home." She said that doesn't seem fair; so finally, she gave what I asked for.

Well, now it's 10:30 a.m. Now I've got money, but I need manpower. I rented a truck with only one man to help. Everybody I knew was tied up today. So finally, my friend started calling some of his partners, and we found 2 by 12:30 p.m. Well, hell! Now Billy's sitting out front. I called the police because now I'm scared. Finally, they came, and said, "As long as he keeps his distance, he was fine." So he's been making a video of everyone who came and went. Other police that knew him from before heard the call and have been stopping by off-and-on. Officer Thomas and I were standing on the porch. He walked right up in front of us and wanted to ask a question about his house. The officer said, "You know you are too close." I came in the house at this point. He videoed the front; then he videoed the back of the house. At 5 p.m. he left only to return a few minutes later with this woman who now sits in front of the house too, as we left with all my flowers they took out the front. And he had the nerve to ask my godsister for the key! She told him my time wasn't up yet. He's going to really act a fool when he finds out my attorney gave me one more day for him bringing the money late.

Called at 9:45 p.m. harassing my godmother, saying I took the fireplace out of the wall in the basement and "She don't have no Order of Protection now." My godmother said, "What do you mean by that?" He shut up. My godmother then told him, "You didn't own anything until she helped you get it." That was the end of the conversation. Called later on about key to house.

6/9/96 - 1 p.m.
Billy called about keys. Celia told him Charlene would be in about 6 p.m. Billy called about 6:30 p.m. We told him he could pick up keys to the house. Billy showed about 7:25 p.m. with 2 policemen. Charlene made him sign receipt for keys like he made her sign for my check.

As I write, you put me out of my home today, as of June 9, 1996. If this ever becomes a book, I'll dedicate this page to my ex-husband, William Harvey, III, Attorney Shaw, and B. E. Starks. You put me through hell today as my mother-in-law, Ms. Gladys Eddy, sat and lied. But I've learned the hard way. Life is a river which flows through many turns and changes. But even when that river takes us in different directions, we will always cross each other again, just around the bend. I'll never forget or forgive you all for this day. But maybe God will when you all finally meet Him. Lord willing, after June 9, I'll find a better home one day.

* *

Last Page
(Written June 10, 1996)

Remember me and other special women—that the 215 Ruling kept my medical records and the fact that I was a battered wife from ever being entered in court in my divorce case May 9, 1996. This was a critical past 2 years for me. So much will be decided, and so much has happened to me that is unjust and unfair. It's my hope that after writing to let everyone know of my story that justice will be done and things will be made right, but I was wrong. As I've told my story open and honestly, most people understood what had happened but could not change things. So in many ways, I feel betrayed. Our legal system had failed me as a battered wife after I followed every step they told me to do. I had poor and improper representation and a serious default in justice from our courts. Then I found a second attorney to hear my story, and he told me I was set up and sold out by my first attorney. The 2nd attorney tried whatever he could to help make right the wrong and to see that justice was done, but the court wouldn't undo the 215 Ruling that went down behind my back in April of '96.

To all my friends who witnessed this madness they put me through, I love you and wanted to say, "Thanks for being there for me" and a special thanks for Attorney Theodore Birndorf. To you all, I have dedicated this book, *My Last Tears.*

Love, Always
Mrs. Deborah B. Harvey

P. S. Even though the court has forsaken us, remember God never will. God would never leave us alone. Always remember that He knows the truth . . .

* *

<u>6/11/96 - 7:15 p.m.</u>
I called my neighbor, Mrs. Baker. She said Billy showed up Sunday 6/9/96, 10 p.m. and as he backed in front of our house, 4 police cars pulled up with guns out. Mrs. Baker said he was trying to explain I wasn't there, and he had papers to be in the house now. I wish I could have been the bug on the wall that night. Well, since I've been out of court and that damn house, my blood pressure has been OK (117/86 or 124/86), but from sleeping on my godmother's couch, my back hurts a lot. Billy still has my insurance intact. I picked up my medicine at Walgreens Monday evening.

<u>6/19/96</u>
Had dentist appt. Teeth cleaned, 2 fillings.

<u>6/22/96 - 10 a.m.</u>
Notes: Things to read to help me through hard times, like right now . . .

> *Lord, grant me the serenity to accept the things I cannot change, the courage to change the things I can and the wisdom to hide the bodies of those people I had to kill because they pissed me off!*

> Rules for Today: *Do nothing that you would not like to be doing when Jesus comes. Go to no place where you would not like to be found when Jesus comes. Say nothing that you would not like to*

be saying when Jesus comes.

You can get in touch with the spiritual by simply being still and calling the names of people who are no longer with us but who are now part of the universe. They are the ancestors and spiritual forces. Just calling their names puts you in touch. Sitting in my backyard surrounded by nature around me brings this peace.

An old saying: "In this life there will be storms"; and "Nobody ever told me that the road would be easy, but I don't believe the Lord has brought me this far to leave me."

A *ship that always sails backward never sees the sunset.* As I divorce soon, I've started to see the sunset again in my life, and it's a good feeling.

The power of spirit is that it's wherever you are. You really can't codify an experience and say, "Well, this is religious, and this is spiritual."

Listen to the wisdom of our wise soul elders on self confidence: *If you take a position that is not popular, you have to be prepared for the kind of criticism that is meted out. If you have confidence in yourself and faith in God, it is amazing how these criticisms do not affect you. Of course, you are hurt because you want to be accepted, but the criticisms don't paralyze you in to inaction.*

On friendship: *Choose friends who know and like you despite whatever happens in your life. Always know who really love you, and cherish those true and precious friends.*

On marriage and happiness: *You find happiness and love through good and rough times. You don't recognize it at the moment. Just listening to the wind blow or the birds sing or watching a sun set over blue waters or a sun set over the mountain top is really a moment of pure joy. When you find this, you'll learn never to be consumed by today's problems. In time, they will work out. Always live each day as it comes.*

Elders in the Black Foot Tribes would say: "For what lies in the dark will come to truth. For those who speak with a pure soul and heart, the truth will always sing the same tune. From a whisper to a scream, the truth will always sing through without changing the words that the winds sing . . ."

6/26/96
Received letter from new attorney. He's working on witness list. He stated in his letter my CTA ins. for CHMO and Dental may be gone. Concerned how Billy has been acting about taking everything from me.

6/26/96
Called clinic. I had started spotting again 6/24/96 about 7:30 p.m. Just had period 6/13/96.

6/27/96
Went to doctor at noon. Due to stress and all I've been through, my body is off cycle. Doctor said may take 2-3 mos. to correct itself. My medical ins. is still good through CTA. I mentioned my vision and spots. Told me to see eye doctor. (Picked up all medicine at Walgreens.)

6/28/96
Made appt. with CHMO Ins. They had me to call Pearle Vision. Gave me appt. for Wed. at 11 a.m. July 3, 1996 at 350 N. Michigan Ave.

NOTE: 10 yrs. married today.

7/3/96
Went to have eyes checked, CHMO - CTA. Went to Pearle Vision, 350 N. Michigan. Every since my head was beat on the floor, I've had bad headaches and trouble with my eyes. Pick up new glasses Monday.

7/5/96
Blood Pressure 129/90. Real bad headache today. Woke up about 6 a.m. For about 15 minutes, I really didn't know where I was. It was scary . . .

P. S. If anything should happen to me before I see you all again, remember this: Before you cry, just try to understand that I am resting safely in the hollow of God's hand. If I could send a message to each one of you, I'd like to say, "Please, now don't you cry for me. I've reached a brighter day. I'll be preparing for you, just like I did before. Just remember all the good times and picnics we shared. I usually worked hard so those picnics were great for all. So lift your hearts and please don't cry. I'll meet you at the door. So before you cry, remember that God alone knows best and He has called me onward and I rest with Him now. So remember, the pain Billy caused me can never hurt me now. I finally found true happiness. I love you all. Bye for now, but I'll see you again . . ."

* *

PART IV - Waiting for the Tide to Turn

ESSENCE & REVLON WOMEN OF STYLE CONTEST
959 W. Walnut St.
Roselle, N. J. 07203
July 14, 1996
1st Draft

My personal style was a very "Classy Lady." I loved my work as an elementary art teacher and being a behavioral manager at Lawrence Hall Youth Service and entertaining at home with family and friends. But for the last 2 1/2 years, I've been in a battle of being a battered wife. Trying to forget the rage of abuse was too much for the mind and body. I almost lost my mind. All I had at times was enjoying my home and all the nature scenes I could create in my backyard (wildlife, flower gardens, all the way to making a small pond area). But my first attorney teamed up with my husband's attorney and sold me out in court. I lost my home and everything I loved most. I do have a new attorney trying to undo what they did. I had lost that Classy Lady a long time ago, staying to myself, never wanting to be with friends for being ashamed of my marriage. But the love of my godparents and friends has brought me a long way. The Classy Lady wants to come out but is afraid of being hurt again.

(Picture taken of Backyard summer of '95.)

Also wrote to *National Enquirer* c/o New Tips, Lantana, FL 33464.

7/24/96
Court date at 9 a.m., Rm 1502, Daley Center. Left home at 7 a.m. headed to court. With me in court, new Attorney Birndorf, Charlene and Celia Ladner, Helen, Anita, and Leola Nelson. I couldn't believe my eyes—my husband showed up with his woman all hugged over him! Billy's lady was stupid; she came to divorce court with the same baseball cap she wore the late night she put smoke bombs twice at my home inside the drop mailbox in the front hall-way. I had this flashback:

> *She was driving a brown station wagon. It was the same car my neighbors said they had seen when someone was watching the house all the time. Billy drove it to pick up a few things from the house. I guess he was trying to sneak up on me because he drove a gray Lincoln. I know because I gave him the last $200.00 he needed to get it! His lady was lucky I didn't know who she was that night with the smoke bombs! The fire department came and looked at the front hallway. It was black in spots. It looked like the house had been on fire. The police wrote up a report; he said some-body was trying to kill me or scare me out the house.*

As we stood before Judge Leiken with the medical records, my new attorney still couldn't prove my stress problem. Well, the Honorable Judge Leiken asked us one more time to try to work things out, so I agreed. I had enough and would settle for $6,000.00, COBRA Ins. and my money in one lump sum or in $500.00-a-month paymts. In the meantime, the Honorable Judge Leiken had placed a phone call to my doctor's office but didn't have any luck finding him. Then William and his attorney turned down my offer, and the judge gave us another court date—Aug. 21, 1996 at 9 a.m. My new attorney, Mr. Birndorf, was very happy about that.

7/25/96
Received letter from Attorney Birndorf on the confusion on court date July 24, 1996 and how sorry we were about it to Dr. Rahman, M.D. He asked Dr. Rahman to please make the next court date Aug. 21, 1996 at 9 a.m., Rm 1502 at Daley Center.

7/26/96
Received order on Prove-Up on a proposed Judgment for Dissolution. Court date 10/1/1996 at 9 a.m.

7/27/96
Vital Clinic called Dr. Rahman; wanted me to come in for review of medical problems. My blood pressure was out of control after May 9, '96 court date.

119

<u>7/29/96 - 2 p.m.</u>
Dr. appointment with Rahman. Due to my nerves being shot, he has put me back in Stress Therapy. I'm waiting on Morgan Park Behavioral Service to call me now about appointment. Chgo. HMO Mental Health Service, 1-847-864-4961.

<u>7/30/96</u>
I went to Merchandise Mart building for CTA Payroll. Talked with Mr. H. Brown on my maintenance check being stopped and when was that order placed. Still nobody knows. I wanted a copy of original stop payment placed May 23, 1996. Nobody has it. I talked to Ms. Jerry Spencer 312-664-7200, Ext. 4534 May 23, 1996.

It was funny this morning when I told Mr. H. Brown, Payroll Supervisor (664-7200, Ext. 4531), who I was and what I wanted, the whole office looked at me as, "Oh, shit! She's back." He looked but still no luck. We got there about 12:30 p.m.

Then we were off to Pearle Vision Express (350 N. Michigan) to have my glasses fixed; then to the Daley Center, 8th floor to records. I wanted to look at my file, Case 94-D-4432. I had a lot of papers stolen in court May 9, 1996, so I wanted to make copies of things I wanted. Boy, did I see a lot of papers Starks had never given me before I fired him! I had 25 pages copied.

<u>8/2/96 - 5 p.m.</u>
Back in Stress Therapy. This time one-on-one. 1701 W. Monterey with Carol Armstrong. (Was in Out-Patient 1 or 2 times a week with Ester Morgan Watts till Nov. '95) 1-312-881-7316. I don't remember much about being partially hospitalized Jan. 1994. Will attend every Friday
5 p.m. Karen Frontezak-Armstrong, Pager (2) 224, Voice mail 312-276-5276.

<u>8/8/96</u>
I wrote reporter Pam Zeikman - Channel 2 News; Walter Jacobson, Channel 32 News; and Fran Speilman, *Chicago Sun-Times Newspaper.*

<u>8/9/96 - 8:45 a.m.</u>
I sleep on my godmother's couch. Boy, last night was rough! We had sprayed the bathroom for gnats and roaches, and one must have fallen from the ceiling in my head. I thought I felt something but didn't see anything in the mirror in my head as I left the bathroom. While about 1 a.m. last night, I was having a dream, this roach was carrying something across my pillow. I wanted to wake up but didn't till it went toward my ear. When I jumped and

slapped the shit out of my face holding whatever in place till I reached the kitchen light, I then saw the roach I'd killed. Every time I try to fall off to sleep, I wake up from a crazy dream of roaches nesting in my head and crawling out of my mouth and nose. I fell off the couch twice. Then I finally put cotton balls in my ears and went to sleep—I guess.

I woke up about 7:30 a.m. trying to figure out what the hell I was feeling in my ears. I forgot about the cotton balls. I jumped straight up looking in the mirror and had to laugh at myself. I told my godsister, Celia, and we had a good laugh. My little godniece looked at both of us like we had lost our marbles.

Well, in a little bit, I'll go mail my packages I put together yesterday.

1:30 p.m. - I went to dentist's office about a doctor's note for the injury to lower jaw from beating to head Nov. 27, 1993. They took new x-ray of teeth. It was time for one.

5:45 p.m. - Just got back from therapy. Karen didn't show, so I just finished leaving her a voice mail. (Ms. June Reddrick dropped me off. Caught bus back home.)

8/21/96
I lost everything in court! Judge Liekien wouldn't let my medical records stand on their own. He needed every doctor there, and only one was free for court date. He (the judge) said I had received mental damage but nothing else. He didn't provide medical care in the divorce and I'm still seeing a therapist. I can only hope the Bar Assn. finds my first attorney, Mr. Starks, wrong for the way he handled my case May 9, 1996. I only got $6,000.00 but not at one time. I'll receive $400.00 in 15 monthly payments from William Harvey when he decides to give it to me. How am I supposed to live and start my life over like the judge told me to do on this?

Fri. 8/25/96
I had another blackout in my memory. I forgot I had told Celia I would go to Kiddieland in Maywood with the kids' Bible class, and I forgot I had my best girlfriend, Helen, dropping her daughter off Friday night to go with us Saturday morning. I was telling Celia I was going to a softball game Saturday, and she turned and looked at me like I had lost my mind. She started yelling, "Don't you remember you said you would go to Kiddieland and Helen is bringing Attia by here tonight?" I just looked and said, "If I said that, I'll do it," and went to make other plans about softball game. I forgot I had therapy today also with Karen Armstrong at the Behavioral Clinic at 5:30 p.m.

121

8/28/96

Ms. Erica Danzee called me twice about my ADA pass from CTA on transportation in their van or cars. She is trying to rush my application through for me. Gave my Social Security number as ID. Ms. Erica's phone # 917-Help. I still haven't heard from the Bar Assn. or Attorney Starks after I sent them more information I found in my divorce files July 30. Also I haven't heard from Channel 2 or 32 or the *Sun-Times* paper where I sent my story. But the funniest thing happened Friday. I almost forgot. CTA sent me another maintenance check for $209.00. I complained about my checks being stopped May 31, 1996.

8/29/96

Today has started great! Everybody healthy. Living over here with my godmother and family has been fun these past few months, and the neighbors are like one big family. Everyone helps each other. My little godniece always wakes up asking everyone, "How was your sleep last night?" which makes my day start with a smile—(although some nights I could kill her godfather, James, who laughs and cleans his room late at night when people are trying to sleep). My godmother, Charlene, is one in a million. She's always there for me, and I'll be there for her. Her daughter, Celia, I love like a real sister. We have been through a lot together. I guess I'm very blessed after all!

9/4/96 - 10:15 a.m.

I called Vital Clinic and talked with Nurse Jean about $500.00 I owe Dr. Rahman for going to court. I told her I'd pay, but no job now.

9/5/96

Called CTA-ADA Service 917-Help for transportation rides and spoke to Erica Danzee at
10:30 a.m. She transferred me to ADA verifier, Ms. Sandra, 917-4367. Sandra gave me my ride ID number P40629. Social Security number was verified at 10:45 a.m. Sept. 5, 1996. All my information will be sent to me in the mail. Can start to use service Sept. 8, 1996. Thank You, Lord! I really needed this. You and I know the ride on buses and trains and long walks through tunnels was too much for me. Thanks again.

I still haven't heard from my ex-husband, William Harvey, III on my 1st paymt. of $6,000.00 he owes me. I'll give him to the 13th of Sept. 1996; then I'll raise holy hell over it!

9/26/96

On Sept. 16, 1996, I received a letter from my new Attorney Birndorf of Just Cause Ruling to return to court Oct. 3, 1996 at 9:30 a.m., Rm 1508 under

Honorable Julian Frazin at the Daley Center because my ex-husband won't pay me my money. I called my granny to go to court with me.

9/27/96
Picked up medicine from Walgreens. Called in for 4 refills 9/23/96.

10/1/96
I wrote Attorney Registration and Disciplinary Commission, Attn. John Cosario again. Told him I was still waiting to hear from him on what Attorney Starks did to my case May 9, 1996.

10/6/96
Mailed off SSI papers to Social Security office. Mailed claim for Crime Victims Department to Jim Ryan, Attorney General Dept.; filing for lost wages against William Harvey, III.

10/10/96
Received letter from Jim Ryan's office. Had to fill out another form to mail in to Crime Victims Dept., 100 W. Randolph St., Chicago, IL 60601-3175.

10/21/96
I wrote the Judicial Inquiry Board on the Honorable Judge Lieken on how he handled my divorce, 100 W. Randolph, Room 14-500, Chgo., IL 60601. This was the last straw since I didn't hear from the Attorney Registration and Disciplinary Commission Office, Case 96-CI-2633, Counsel John R. Cosario after I wrote him on information I mailed Aug. of 1996.

10/20/96
Went to doctor's office. Still having trouble with back, balance, and my blood pressure. Gave me 4 refills on my medicine.

10/23/96
Court at 9:30 a.m. Court started late. Both attorneys agreed to continue to Nov. 13, 9:30 a.m., Rm 1508, Judge Frazin. My attorney had a kidnap case waiting in his office. William claimed my money would start around Nov. 15.

10/28/96
Received a letter from Crime Victims Compensation Act. They are reviewing my paperwork for an extension of time of filing so late. Also received letter from Judicial Inquiry Board on ruling of my divorce May 9 and Aug. 21, 1996 by Judge Lieken, Rm 1502.

<u>11/13/96</u>
Had court this morning at 9:30 a.m. Attorney Birndorf asked that my money from William come from his check from Aug. 21 to now. I only received $190.00 of the $6,000.00 I'm due at $400.00 a month. Billy was outside in lobby. His attorney didn't show. The judge agreed to have money come from his check but didn't agree to late charges. Attorney Birndorf said he would try for late charges later with his fee included. As we left court, Billy said, "Is it over?" Attorney Birndorf said, "Is that Billy?" I said, "Yes" to both, looking from left to right. Celia answered Billy also, "Yes, you dummy" and laughed out loud. Billy and his attorney had lied and twisted things their way since April '96 till Celia said, "About time things turned around the right way!"

<u>11/14/96 - 5 p.m.</u>
Celia came from getting the mail out of the box and passed me. Then she returned saying, "These look like checks, but the address was wrong." So I looked, and sure enough, it was 3 checks dated funny. The street was spelled wrong with the wrong zip code. They came from Ohio somewhere. My name was in my maiden name, which I haven't used since 1983. At William's request, I carried Brisco-Harvey since then—plus the check was a 2-party check! He had "in care of Charlene Ladner" (my godmother) on them. He is trying to piss me off, and it's working!

<u>11/15/96 - 11 a..m.</u>
I went to currency exchange and made copies of checks and envelopes and faxed them to my attorney's office. Then I mailed all 3 checks to my bank.

<u>11/25/96</u>
Attorney Birndorf's secretary called to tell me we had court Wed. (11/26/96) at 9:30 a.m., Rm 1508 and for me to be on time because my attorney would be late.

<u>11/26/96</u>
I showed at 9:25 a.m., checked in, and told them my attorney would be late. About 10:55 a.m. we went before the judge, and we lost. He said since my checks were started now, that's all that matters. My late fees were denied for Aug., Sept., and Oct., and he denied Billy paying any of my attorney fees; so my $6,000.00 will be paid in $400.00 mo. paymts. Aug. money I may never receive because he left it up to Billy's side to check into the check I received late from CTA on my maintenance money. The judge did say if my money was stopped before I went to court May 9, 1996, I was owed that check, and they would have to pay me my Aug. payment due me.

Professional services

	Hrs/Rate	Amount
10/18/96- prior itemized billing:		3,063.84
10/23/96- court: could not wait to have the case recalled to have a withholding order entered; respondent in court with his attorney, said the August payment was short because client received an erroneous extra payment on her maintenance; has given his affairs to a consolidator who will pay out on the fifteenth of November; told him not paying the September or October payments not acceptable and late payment of November not acceptable	0.75 200.00/hr	
- phone call client: client went to CTA payroll, talked to H. Brown 664-7200x4531 who says that the late payment that she received was the payment due May 4	0.25 175.00/hr	
11/2/96- letter client: court is November 13	0.25 175.00/hr	
11/13/96- court: judge said would enter order for $400 monthly withholding order, nothing on arrears; left at 10:20, no other attorney; order prepared; returned at noon with order to find order dismissing the petition on the basis of full compliance with the judgment	0.75 200.00/hr	
- court clerk's office: set new motion	0.25 200.00/hr	
- dictate: notice of motion and motion to vacate order of November 13	0.50 175.00/hr	
- dictate: notice of motion and petition for attorney's fees	0.50 175.00/hr	
- discovery: 214 and 237(b) notices	0.25 175.00/hr	
11/14/96- letter client: court is November 26	0.25 175.00/hr	
11/15/96- fax received client: yesterday she received three $400 checks	0.10 175.00/hr	

	Hrs/Rate	Amount
11/18/96- review mail other attorney: copy of order of	0.10	
November 13	175.00/hr	
11/20/96- court clerk's office: motion to vacate filed	0.25	
	200.00/hr	
- review mail client: executed fee petition	0.10	
	175.00/hr	
11/21/96- court clerk's office: filed petition for fees	0.25	
	200.00/hr	
11/22/96- letter other attorney: I will be a little late on the 26th	0.25	
	175.00/hr	
11/26/96- court: request for withholding order denied	0.75	
	200.00/hr	

Total of services and costs:	*5.55*	*$4,110.09*

12/24/96- on account		($100.00)

Balance due		*$4,010.09*

Well, I'm going to write the Attorney General's office and thank them for nothing. I wrote them for help on the way things went down, and I still haven't heard from them. So my case is buried like so many other battered wives . . .

12/2/96 - 10:30 a.m.
Had appointment with psychiatrist, Howard E. Wolin, M. D. Ltd., 233 E. Erie, Chgo. 60611, Suite 808, 312-987-4377. Charlene was going to drive me downtown, but when we went to go gas up her van, we pulled off from station at Vermont and something, and the van stopped. She couldn't get it started. Finally after 45 min., I tried and got it to a vacant lot, where we sat about 10 min.; then it started, but it was too late for me to make doctor apptmt. Sat by Bureau of Disability Office. Call for new date Dec. 4, '96, 9:30 a.m.

12/3/96
Well, this is the first Dec. since moving to Chicago from Charleston, W. VA at age 19 in Sept. of '69 that I have never had a roof of my own over my head at Christmas time. All I do is feel sad and cry on the way the system handled my divorce, leaving me with nothing. I hate my 1st attorney, B. E. Starks, and my ex-husband.

2 p.m. today, I have to meet with Public Aid at 119th and Halsted for receiving food stamps and medical card. Ms. Simons and I had it out about all the questions she was asking. Finally, I got mad and told her to forget the whole thing. Then she asked was I married, and I hit the roof! I said, "Just forget it!" and started to cry. "I don't want to talk about it." As I started to leave, her supervisor came in to see what all the noise was about. I said, "I can't go through this. Just cancel and let me go." Finally, they calmed me down, and we finished everything. But they wrote me up as a depressed, very depressed, battered wife.

12/4/96
Went to see psychiatrist, Dr. Wolin, 312-987-4377, 233 E. Erie, Rm 808, today 9:30 a.m. This was scary. We entered his office, and it was a large room with a black sofa to the left wall, a table and chairs at big picture window straight in front of me, and a desk and chair to my right, with a chair by the door. He reached behind me to turn the light off. I looked behind me and watched. Then he said, "Have a seat by the door." He went across the room and sat at table and chair in front of window. I asked if he wanted my papers and medicine I was on. He said, "No." Then he got a pad and started asking questions. I was fine until he asked me to explain how I got injured. I tried to explain, but I fell apart. It was a sad meeting. After we talked for about 20 mins., I left. (Received apptm. papers Nov. 22, 1996.)

12/5/96

Called Medical Vital Clinic on 96th and Halstd. at 11:50 a.m. Talked with RN Jean Hill. Need something for the flu I have. She advised buy something from drug store because my HMO Ins. there of my ex-husband's CTA job was cut this month. So I should call Monday and transfer from there to a free clinic. This is one year I'll be glad when it is over. Everything that could go wrong and some has gone wrong! And everybody wonders why I'm sad all the time. Personally, I'm ready to kill I'm so mad!

2:45 p.m. - Went to P.O. Box. Received another appointment letter from the Bureau of Disability. P.O. Box 19250, Springfield, IL 62794-9250.

12/6/96

I called Dr. Howard E. Wolin, M. D.'s office, 111 N. Wabash Ave. (Suite 702) Chgo. 60602 (312-787-7077). Spoke to his secretary, Ms. Arlene, at 9:20 a.m. about new papers to see Dr. Wolin again. She said I only had to make one appointment and that was on Dec. 4. I asked her about me forgetting to give him this form I had. Arlene said they had their own copy. I mailed the copy of Nov. 25's appointment papers in with the Dec. 4 appointment date I made to Adjudicator: Gerald Coffman (800-225-3607. Ext. 58196). I also mailed medicine sheet on 4 of them to Mr. Gerald Coffman.

12/7/96

Controlling pain without medicine begins with positive thinking. Nothing makes me feel better, and when I'm relaxed, my pain begins to ease. I know I'll always be in pain. It's been with me since Nov. 27, 1993, but with the medicine I'm on, it gives me the power to reduce my pain at its worse, and sometimes I can bear the pain without the medicine. Some days I feel that the pain takes over my life, but I can't allow this. I know I'm a victim of being a battered wife and the scars and hurt are deep. I can only fight to control the pain and hurt so I can start to live my life again somehow. With God's help, my life will have meaning again—one day soon. (5:53 p.m.)

12/9/96 - 11:20 p.m.

I wrote the *Sun-Times* paper a 300-word essay on memories of 1996 on my story, "What Order of Protection?" May 9 . . . Had to be in by Dec. 20, 1996. Notes included "Backpage."

* *

My Last Tears Will Be My Memories of 1996

I regret the court system failed me as a battered wife. Mar. '96, I was really looking forward to this 2-yr. court battle finally coming to an end. May 7, I was told I had a court date May 9 to receive date for my trial, where all my medical records and witness list had to be in. To my surprise, I ended up in court having my trial without any of the above brought up to help win my case. I got sick and freaked out on what took place. So after it was all over, I couldn't believe my attorney had set me up. So I called around and told my story. I had police records, pictures, and medical records to prove I was battered to get a 2-yr. Order of Protection. But all of this was not in my divorce. I couldn't figure out why. I hired another attorney who tried to undo the wrong. He couldn't. He found out the 1st attorney had misdiaried my court dates in April, and my husband's attorney had filed a paper that said my medical records and things weren't in and that they could never be entered. So as my 2nd attorney tried to help me, my 1st attorney sat with my husband and his attorney. I got more under my Order of Protection than in my divorce. I had my home, maintenance money, insurance, and my husband paid the mortgage note. I lost all of this in my divorce.

I've been under doctor's care since Nov. 27, 1993. How am I supposed to start over? I applied for disability, food stamps, and medical card. I've told my story to the Attorney General's office and the Judicial Inquiry Board. I still haven't heard anything since my last letters in Sept.

As I think back on 1996, I stood before a judge May 9 who didn't even know I was a battered wife. I asked for an extension on my Order of Protection, and as he looked at both attorneys and back at me with tears in my eyes, he said, "What Order of Protection? Nobody told me about that . . ."

There is no justice for battered wives, even when they follow the guidelines to the end. We lose! So I'll remember '96 for the rest of my life. I just wanted to thank all the people who were there by my side and helped me. Thank you very much for everything.

Deborah Brisco-Harvey
Dec. 9, 1996 - 11:20 p.m.

* *

<u>12/14/96 - 9:30 p.m.</u>
Well, I worked for Kelly Temp last 2 days, and my back feels like shit. I just stood up off of the couch to answer door to let my godmother, Charlene, in and caught a pain in my back that hurt so I fell to the floor. Well, also it is Dec. 14, and I haven't received my 4th check from Billy as of today for $400.00. How in the hell did the court think I was supposed to live! One of the police officers that keeps up with me called to see how I was. I told him about the divorce. Officer Thomas said with all the stuff on my husband, there was no way I should have lost my case. He said Billy must have paid through the ass when he bought my 1st attorney off. Then he said the system was designed that way—for people with money. He also said every dog has its day . . . .

My nerves are bad again. I've started picking sores all over my face, arms, and stomach again in my sleep. If I haven't heard anything from the Attorney General's office by Jan. 1, 1997, I'm going to write the Attorney General's office in Washington, D. C., Ms. J. Reno. Since the court left me homeless and broke, I ran across this saying that fit me: "Most of us don't live within our income because we don't consider that living"; or "It's called take-home pay because there's no other place you can afford to go with it." Oh well, that's my laugh therapy for the year.

<u>12/16/96</u>
Tonight there was a good movie on TV, "To Stand Against Fear." It gives me hope in my fight against what the legal system did to me and reminds me that I have to keep fighting against the odds because there is no justice for battered or assaulted wives. Meanwhile, today one of the companies I'd work for as a temp may hire me, if I can pass drug test.

<u>12/20/96</u>
Thinking back to May 9, 1996 as I drink my coffee this morning, I remember trying to defend my cause since my attorney, Mr. Starks, wasn't saying anything to help me out. This is when I realized he had jumped sides on me. Judge Lieken had no kind words toward me. All he kept saying was, "Speak when you're asked a question." As I tried to tell what was going on, he yelled louder and louder till finally I said something that shut him up about my Order of Protection being extended till the judgment came in. Then he yelled at both attorneys, "What Order of Protection! No one told me about that."

Well, to make a short story here, I'm reading an article I should send Judge Lieken, Rm 1502, at the Daley Center—"Think and Listen Before You Speak." *Kind words spoken to a person can lift their spirits even in the worse of times and encourage them with some hope. Cruel words, on the other hand, can crush their spirits and literally destroy them* (like the court system did me). *A person's tongue is like a sword.* I wish I could sue the judge for mental harassment and emotional distress. *Unfortunately, the wound that it leaves can't be closed with stitches or a bandage. These wounds are internal and sometimes never heal.* Like my mom always said, "If you can't find something good to say to someone, it's good to say nothing at all when you don't have all the facts to judge a person who's trying to tell you something . . ."

To the court system and attorneys that left me with nothing in my divorce: You even took back what I started with.

> Dear Santa,
>
> Send them all a note saying your gift was too large to fit in the box I couldn't afford to buy to put it in, so I decided to tell my story to all I meet about what you did to me . . . .
> P. S. Santa, I may forgive one day, but I'll never forget.
>
> Love,
> Debby

12/25/96
The good and pain of ending a 14-yr. marriage: Remembrance is like a candle. Shines brightest at holiday time. I'm going to take it very, very slow in the love and marriage deptment. It's been 3 yrs now. Maybe by next Xmas, I'll find a man, and I'll pick him like the old folks did with Xmas trees—tall, very fresh, and makes you light up every time you see him, with a smile . . . Oh, well, maybe the perfect gift will come along before I'm 99.9 years old. (Smile)

Xmas day was great. I spent it with my godmother and family. I videoed Xmas morning with the kids.

1/1/97
Happy New Year. Boy, what a beginning! My back and left leg are killing me. How can I forget what Billy did when the pain is with me morning, noon, and night! I still haven't heard from Crime Victims Compensation, Bureau of Disability, Judicial Inquiry Board, or the Attorney General's office. Living in the street with no money, support is hard. How much can one person take? I hope somebody will hire me soon, with all my medicine and medical problems. My bills are so far behind. I finally got food stamps in Dec. '96 but no medical card yet. Everybody has all the information they need, so I don't know what the holdup is . . .

1/2/97 - 10:30 a.m.
I needed to go to the store, so I decided to walk. After 3 blocks, my lower back went out, and down I went! A nice lady driving by stopped and helped me up. I thanked her and kept going. I'm so scared that one day it's going to go out for good.

1/18/97
Received more papers from Illinois Department of Disability. I've got another doctor's appt. 1/23/97 11:30 a.m. at Health Evaluation Center, 111 N. Wabash Ave. Suite 1414 312-606-9200.

1/24/97
Well, since I can't get help from anywhere, I'm forcing myself to go back to work. My back hurts so bad at times till my leg and feet hurt with each step. I've got to try to keep going because I can't win for losing. Public Aid and Social Security disability can't help me, and the court system threw me out with nothing!

New Idea
Submitted by Deborah Brisco-Harvey 1/28/97

Jan. 24, 1997 I missed Shuttle Van by 2 minutes. Shuttle left River Rd. 7:35 p.m. I arrived 7:37 p.m. I waited from 4:57 p.m. to 5:44 p.m. for a 115th St. bus. Due to bad weather, the shuttle van has waited for up to 11 minutes for late riders. But the one day I'm late, it only waited 5 minutes. This is not fair! I'm always on time, and I missed a whole night's pay for 2 minutes! I've called CTA to complain about the bus run, but this won't pay me for money lost on my paycheck. I've got a bad back, and it takes a lot out of me to travel that distance for nothing.

I can't win for losing.

* **

Submit to Wesley & Jessen
"New Idea Box"

Shuttle van needs to have a late grace period of 15 minutes on bad-weather days, 10 minutes on other days.

7:30 p.m. River Rd pick-up doesn't have any busses running after this time. I leave home from 116th & Carpenter at 4:55 p.m. giving myself time for 2 busses:

115th Morgan bus	Rosemont L.
5:07 p.m.	6:59 p.m.
5:22 p.m.	7:15 p.m.
5:38 p.m.	7:31 p.m.

* *

2/6/97
My back went out again. Still hurt real bad.

2/15/97 - 6 p.m.
No check from Billy Harvey.

2/18/97
I'm in the process of finding me a place to live now. I'm dealing with Market Street Mortgage Co. 8752-3 W. 159th St., Orland Park, IL 60462. The mortgage co. is willing to give me a loan for a home in the amount of $54,900.00 price range.

2/20/97 - 11:30 a.m.
I called Check Fee Service in Columbus Ohio; they said the last check was sent 1/15/97 and there wasn't one scheduled to go out for Feb. He had stopped it. I called on my calling card to verify I really did, if needed later. Then I called my second attorney, Mr. Birndorf. He wants me to send him last paperwork to take him back to go to court again. Still haven't heard from disability office on SSI checks.

2/28/97
Billy sent a check for $3,220.00. Still owes me $590.00. I wrote his attorney about the last of the money.

3/8/97 - 3 p.m.
It's been a while since I've written in my diary. But yesterday was a long day. I've gone back to work now 3 days one week and 4 days the next. The company, Wesley & Jessen, is real nice to work for, but my back and legs hurt so bad till some days I come home with tears in my eyes from the pain I'm in. I'm going to lie down now and take my medicine. Maybe I'll feel better tomorrow.

3/9/97 - 7:45 a.m.
I had a bad night. The pain was really bad. I was awaken by a bad pain in my lower right back and a muscle spasm that kept my right leg raising up and

down, and I couldn't get control for about 2 minutes. Then I just got up and started writing again.

3/10/97
A new year and new thoughts:

We can complain because roses have thorns, or be glad because thorns have roses. (This is <u>man</u> in my life.)

4/2/97
I got so sick at work till I don't know how I made it home. My back went out on me for 2 days. Had to go to the doctor.

4/27/97
Well, for the last 2 mos. I've been house-looking. I finally found one, and the loan and everything went through last Wed., so today I'm going for my final walk-through the house at 4 p.m. Closing is supposed to be April 30, '97 at 10:30 a.m.

4/30/97 - 10:45 a.m.
Closing on house was smooth. My attorney, Mr. Grossman, said I really got a great deal on everything. I always talk with Mr. Grice, but his wife was at closing. Boy, did we have a surprise! It was my ex-sister-in-law, Penny. Well, we stopped closing for a second and had family reunion catch-up news on the last 15 yrs. (My 1st marriage only lasted 1 1/2 yrs . . . . Alan played the horses too much and always lost everything we had . . .) But we finally closed about 12:45 p.m. They still have a lot to move out of the house. Both won't be finished till Sunday or Monday before I get keys.

My knee I fell on a few months ago when my back went out on me is still hurting. Today it's big, like an extra knot on the side of it. I could kill my ex-husband, William, for the pain he left me with and got away scot-clean in court! One day, he will pay!

I've found a lot of new programs to write to tell my story to this year. Somewhere, somebody will listen and tell it for me. (7:30 p.m.)

P. S. I did have a nice surprise. After closing, my real estate lady, Ms. Dorothy Lott, took me out to lunch and thanked me for choosing them for getting my 1st home with. She was a beautiful person to work with on this deal we closed on. And Mike and Barbara of Market Street Mortgage Company were great with me too.

My new home is located at 12131 S. Wallace—3 bdrm upstairs and bath, kitchen, dining rm and living rm, then full basement, nice yard, (no flowers or trees), new 2 1/2 car garage with patio. It's an old house with small front porch, which I love. Can't wait to start working on it and moving in soon.

5/2/97

I called the phone company to have my old phone number turned on in the house. Also called the light and gas company and wrote the water company as they requested. So now I don't have to worry about that. Ex-owner called to give me their code on alarm system till I get it changed over in my name next week. They will be moving Fri., Sat., and Sunday. Should get keys by Monday or late Sunday.

* *

SHELTER FROM THE STORM

SHELTER FROM THE STORM CONTINUES

(My goddaughter, Johanna among the flowerbeds)

Deborah Brisco-Harvey

Happy Fathers Day
(Written May, 1997)

Do you have any idea how much you've changed my life? Sometime I feel like a flower opening up beneath the golden warmth of your love, responding to the sunshine that the very sight of you brings. That's how safe I feel with you. It's a wonderful feeling made all the more special because I know this is just the beginning of the understanding and trust we will share. For with time, I want to know you completely.

I want to give all of myself to you, holding nothing back except for the mystery that allows us to be two separate people, joined by one beautiful love. Tony, this past year has been wonderful. I feel as though I've been running through a wildflower field, with my feet floating among the soft white clouds, surrounded by a perfect blue sky. So let me take this time to say thanks for being there for me, for you make me feel all the above with each time we share together.

Kiss Kiss and Hug
Love Ya!

10/9/97 - 3:40 a.m.
Well, at work, I've decided assholes like I was married to shouldn't walk away with everything in a battered wife divorce and the court stand by and amen it without ever seeing my facts or hearing my side of anything. That's why my story must be told! I still have nightmares about my beating. And the pain I'm in most of the time at work, I wouldn't wish on the worst dog I've known (which is him, by the way).

People at work laugh at the way I walk and move sometimes. It's so hard. When I think of the pain I'm in, I just cry myself to sleep everyday hoping I'll win the lottery so I won't have to go back there to work. But the lottery's out for people like me. So I'll probably cry myself to sleep a-many more days. Since I've been back to work, part of my time is spent trying to avoid paperwork. Every since my head was beat on the floor, my vision hasn't been the same. Sometime it really scares me.

Don't Give Up (1/1/98)

I gave up on love after 14 yrs. But don't you give up on love. One day, somewhere, there is a place for you and me and love again. Just don't give up on me yet. Some days are so lonely since our breakup. But I'm trying to make each new day count for something. I know it's never been easy. But there's a place where I belong, since a new river is flowing my way. With a gentle flow of warm water for me to rest upon. He's proud of who I am, and my heart has a place where I belong now. So to all of you that have given up, fight each new day like it's your last. And don't give up because new rivers are born everyday. I know I've found the most gentle river ever named Tony M. So don't give up on love.

NEVER GIVE UP ON LOVE

Friends Forever!

Friends Forever!

3/1/98 - 10:30 p.m.
When I arrived home, I got a hell of a pain in my back as I reached the front stairs of my porch. I felt my body go faint. Finally, I got myself together and got into my home, only to find I had fallen, hit my steps, and injured my face right under my nose, causing me pain in my front tooth. So I took pain medicine and went to bed.

3/2/98 - 7:30 a.m. & 3/3/98
My mouth was twice its normal size, my eyes all puffy. The pain in my back was still there. I just took more pain medicine till finally March 3rd I ended

140

up in the dentist's office where they had to cut me under my lip to drain it to get my eyes from closing. They gave me more medicine, and I'll need more work done later. You know, the court left me with nothing in my divorce due to the 215 Ruling that kept all my information about my injuries from being a battered wife and under Order of Protection from my husband from the new judge I went before. Now I wish I had killed him when I had the chance. When I called 911 and was yelling for help, I should have shot him then instead of waiting for the police to write assault charges as he threatened me in front of them. If I had shot him like I wanted, at least justice would have been served!

3/22/98

You know, it's been almost two years those 2 attorneys ruined my battered wife divorce case, and I can't forget it. I guess a battered wife always has to remember her limitation as to what the law is all about. And there is no justice for us—when we are down and beaten, can't work; no-good husband can buy off no-good attorneys a dime a dozen to win their case, especially with the 215 Ruling that gets to keep all your battered case and medical records from ever entering the divorce case.

You know, Mar. '96, I had the perfect plan to kill my husband off. As I slept on our sofa couch, he always entered the door with a rage of anger that would wake the dead. As I lay there with my gun and phone, at the sound of his key in the front door, I would dial 911. As the phone lay by my side, 911 would hear the raging man threaten me, and as he got closer and closer, I'd scream and then unload my gun till his voice was no more. Now that would have been justice well done!

But now, it's all over, and my search for justice through the court system was a waste of time. To all battered women: When you have that chance, kill the asshole! For that's the only way to win. I sit with pain throughout my body. The pain won't let me forget what happened to me.

PART V - Potpourri

(Songs, Letters, Poems, Etc.)

My Article Published in Nature Society News, June 1992

* *

"My Last Tears"
June 9, 1998

SPECIAL NOTE: Whitney Houston has to sing this song in my movie. She knows the inside pain. I hear it in her songs at times.

Honey, why didn't you leave when I asked you to.
Honey, the pain is too much. I didn't mean to do it.
Baby, now that you are gone, I don't have to sing the inside sad blues anymore.

My Last Tears

I was hurting, honey—hurting, honey—on the inside as well as out.
But since you been gone, I know it was wrong.
But the hurt has gone.
Since I stopped my pain, I won't cry no more.
My blues are gone in the whispers of the cold nights.
I used to fear when you were alive.
I won't cry no more inside.
Sad blues songs. The hurt blues is gone.
I know I love you, but the hurt had to end.
My love, the only way I knew how.
I have no more tears.
My last tears are gone in the whispers of the night.

* *

My Tee Shirt
June 9, 1998

FRONT OF TEE SHIRT:
    Bold Letters
    My Last Tears

BACK OF TEE SHIRT:
    My submission and quietness
    Were not your victory.
    But instead, the inner
    Strength of my pen & paper
    Will be your defeat.

Color: Royal Blue with white outline

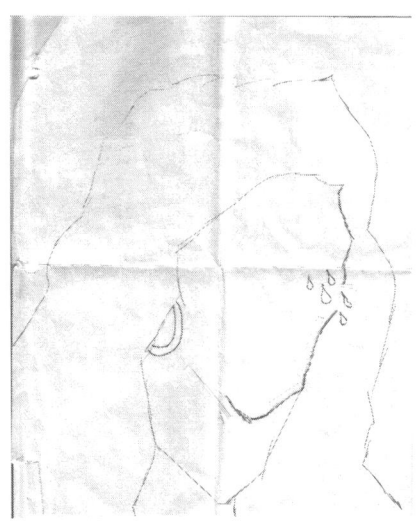

* *

Letter to Oprah
July 30, 1998

Dear Oprah,

Please let this be one of those letters you read. I've written a novel called *My Last Tears*. I'm a battered wife that went through the devil's back door in Nov.

143

'93 down to nothing. And now, I'm just reaching the steps of heaven's gates. And I can't start to climb yet because there's something hanging in the back of my mind . . .

The 2nd attorney I hired was my guardian angel, Theodore Birndorf, who went to bat for me but couldn't undo what they had done. His last words were, "Keep writing. You have one of those true stories that should be told." All my friends told me to write you to see about help with my book. It's in rough form and needs work. I've all the papers to prove it, and I've written a lot of people who wish I would drop it, but I can't. The divorce judge I went before didn't even know I was a battered wife.

Thanks for taking the time to read this.

> From:
> I'm trying to climb God's stairway
> Debby B. Harvey

* *

Letter to Chicago Abused Women Coalition
P.O. Box 477916
Chgo. 60647-7916
Feb. 21, 2000

Dear CAWC,

I was a physically and emotionally abused person. I finally made up my mind to get out and went for a 2-yr Order of Protection after my husband threatened me in front of the judge. The police officers in my neighborhood were great. They told me I didn't have to live like this and gave me information on the Pro Bono Advocates.

Everything I won I lost in the end. My attorney sold out. I really feel he did. I got to court; I couldn't have my witnesses. My medical reports and pictures of injuries were not allowed in my divorce. I finally called my Pro Bono attorney and told him what was happening. He agreed to look into it and told me to go and look at my files. There were a lot of things I was seeing for the 1st time. That's when I saw the 215 Ruling that kept all my information from ever going to court. The Pro Bono attorney tried hard to undo the mess that was made, but the judge let the 215 stand. So my attorney told me I had a story to tell, and I tell it everywhere. So I would love information on volunteer work or talking with women. They sent me through hell, but I'm coming back stronger than before.

144

Thanks for listening. It still hurts a lot.

Debby B. Harvey

* *

Letter to Ill. Coalition Against Domestic Violence
March 15, 2000

Dear Ill. Coalition against Domestic Violence,

I received a handbook some time ago from the nice police officer that helped me through a rough time. They told me that I didn't have to live the way I was. I read the book and finally made that 1st step out. I had enough of the threats and being beat. I was damned if I did and damned if I didn't.

I went through the Pro Bono Advocates to win a 2-yr. Order of Protection. But when I went for my divorce, everything—medical records, police reports, witnesses—was kept from crossing my divorce judge's desk because of the 215 Ruling. I lost everything because of it. How can the court set up rules for us to go by, and on the other hand, take it from us with a 215 Ruling? I used to believe in the system, but I don't anymore. My attorney through the Pro Bono Program was great—Attorney Theodore Birndorf. But I couldn't afford him for my divorce, so I went with someone I could pay. But he lost everything! I had called Mr. Birndorf crying, trying to tell him what happened. He felt sorry for me and took my cause and tried to undo the wrong that happened. But the judge would not overturn the 215 Ruling. If I'm a battered wife and my divorce case depends on all this information and I'm the one who filed for the divorce, tell me how can a judge let a 215 Ruling keep it out!

How do women like me fight to get rid of the 215 Ruling and keep it from ever being involved in a battered wife divorce case ever again? Until some-one tells me how and the wrong is undone, I'll never believe in the court sys-tem again. Help me to have faith again.

Waiting to hear from you. Thanks for listening.

* *

Deborah Brisco-Harvey

Note About Writing to Metro Briefs
Re: Grand Jury Subpoenas File From Judge's Divorce Case
April 28, 2000

I wrote Metro Briefs to see if they had more information on this case because I think it's wrong for temporary judges to make final decisions on cases of 2 yrs. in one day. This is how I lost my case . . .

* *

Mr. Shade
Sept. 10, 2000 - 8 a.m.

The Shadow of my life came at a low point. He's also there to open a gate, a door, or carry my bags to my door. You never see his whole face, but his body is built like he lives in a gym. The Shadow is never there when you look for him, but if you are in need, he's always there. Even in the winter time after a big or little snow, I can see him walk away from my gate as I approach my sidewalks and steps, which look like snow has never touched them. The Shadow softly looks back as I close my gate. I gently wave goodbye wishing he would stay awhile.

As we gather at Xmas time in the park to sing of joy we had all year, the Shadow passes by as we all look and wonder will he join us this time, never showing his face as he moves on down the way. I've tried to put a name to Shadow, but Tom, Joe, or Will just don't fit. Then in a dream, the perfect name came. (My aunt passed some time ago, but she's always in my dreams.) As my Aunt Nellie and I sat in the park, and as the soft winds flowed through the tall tree above, and as the winds sang their song, my aunt started to leave. She looked back at me and said, "You should call him 'Mr. Shade.'" As I woke this new day, I still remember the name she told me. So I had to write this poem about the man in my life with no name.

* *

A Battered Wife's Divorce
(Idea for Movie of My Story)
Nov. 2000

Suppose book is published and somehow a tough top attorney reads the book and decides to put all the facts before a really true courtroom to see just how the divorce case would have gone if it had gone to trial.

* *

MY SONG
"Oh!!! I Still Remember"
June 28, 2002

Oh! Lord, why do I still have that man in my mind and heart . . .
Lord knows all he put me through, I shouldn't even remember his name,
But I remember, all so well, the good and bad time so often.
Oh! Lord, all the pain, hurt and wrong he caused,
Oh, I shouldn't even remember his name,
But I still remember after all this time.
Oh! the pain he left my body with will remain always.
Oh! Lord, please tell me why do I still have that man on my mind and heart.
Lord knows, all Billy put me through, I shouldn't even remember his name.
Oh! when will my heart and mind just let it all go . . .
Oh! I shouldn't even remember his name.
Oh, my. I shouldn't remember his name.
Lord knows I shouldn't remember.
Oh, when will my heart and mind just let go?
Just let go, let it all go, just let go.
Oh, Lord, when . . . (repeat)

* *

"Express yourself completely, then keep quiet." Lao-Tzu

* *

"Feathers and Wings Rule This Far South Side Chicago Kingdom"
(My Article published in *Nature Society News, June 2002*)

Dear *Nature Society News*. Each year just gets better and better. I am in the National Wildlife Federation's Backyard Habitat Program. Feathers and Wings rule the south side kingdom here.

It's taken me a long five years of planting, hanging bird and butterfly homes, digging small water holes and placing feeders everywhere. Now it blooms from spring to fall. I'm finally proud of my hard work I've done.

Even my neighbors are asking me, "I saw a bird that looked like [this]; what did I see?"

I just smile and look like I'm thinking for a few minutes, then say, "You saw a common Yellowthroat; the man [male] has a mask across his face."

I grew up in Charleston, West Virginia. My parents had beautiful flowerbeds and garden each year.

So my little house on the far south side of Chicago is like walking through to fields of the country.

I really enjoy watching my feathered friends—hummingbirds, goldfinches, chickadees, butterflies—and the bumblebees have a ball around here.

This year I even found a snake enjoying the cool watering hole.

I just wanted to drop a few words. I hadn't written in awhile. Please keep up the great work. I love reading my *News* paper. I hope this year will be great for everyone.

* *

My Blues Song
"The Dog Gets Love"

You came home with rib tips for the dog.
And asked me if I wanted the bread.
Well, the dog ate better than me,
But that's all right.
I still keep your bed clean and your clothes.
I don't know who she is,
But my heart's getting lonely.
Let me tell you the man I want in my life.
He should be like the sunshine above.
Make love to me till I can't take no more.
You see, the man I want in my life
Is a Natural man.
No foolishness in his bone.
Never putting me in the middle of a three-way mess.
You see, when I give my love,
It's all or nothing.
So let me say:

My Last Tears

"Keep feeding the dog better than me."
You're going to miss me one day.
A natural woman is hard to find.
You and the dog will miss me when I'm gone,
And it's not going to take too much longer for that.

* *

PART VI - Seeing the Sunset Again

May 1, 2008 – Love with a Twist

When you love someone that brings you flowers every week, that can look at you in your worst of pain and when you are sick and he still says, "You look great; I'm here for you; let me take care of you for awhile," THAT'S LOVE!

That's "love with a twist" and not "twisted love"! FLASHBACK — 12 years with Billy, who would come home drunk, high or something, who beat me up calling me by another woman's name—Julia—while explaining that he had a good wife. I kept saying over and over, "I'm your wife, Deborah! Remember?" Well, after 20 minutes, he let me go. But that's not the end. He said, "Get in my way, I'll do it again"!

Billy wanted to move on with his life with a younger woman. I told him, "Get out! I'm not going anywhere," while thinking about all the co-signing I did for our home and planting flowers in the front and back yard. When the court removed him from our home, I had to fix the roof and repair the kitchen and hallway to the basement, clean our bedroom ceiling of old insulation and put in new insulation. (I didn't patch the ceiling, but it looked good.) His last words to me were that I was too old—I'm only 4 years older than he is—and I couldn't help him anymore. One day he will eat those words! My heart and mind were left at a "PO'ed" level while I walked into dinosaur stuff. We all know that was one mile high and wide.

The court system left me in the middle with no way out.

It's been 10 yrs since Billy said that, but I've found out I'm **not** old and I **do** look great!

I did go to a mental health clinic for 1 ½ years; I had a total breakdown and was even locked up for a month. I'm still on daily medication. Every night I pray the Lord will remove what happened to me from my heart and mind. Lord knows I re-live the whole thing every night and during the day. So I'm asking everybody to pray with me at night. With a little luck, it might come true.

* *

There hath no temptation taken you but such as is common to man: but God is faithful, who will not suffer you to be tempted above that ye are able; but will with the temptation also make a way to escape, that ye may be able to bear it (I Corinthians 10:13 KJV).

* *

My new life is great! Tony is always there for me. Every summer, I watch him play pro-softball.

We go to Delaware every year to visit his mom and dad, his daughter, Angie, and the 3 grandchildren. I thank God every night for them being in my life now and also for family and friends.

153

I don't work anymore—I'm on disability now since 2004. Billy still owes me a little money he didn't pay. But as it stands, I'll never marry again. Well, if I live to be 90, I'll start looking around; and when I reach 99, I'll say "I do" again. The way I feel with 2 metal plates in my left arm, having had surgery on my right shoulder to have a bone filed down, and with left knee and lower back going out, bad headaches and blurred vision from having my head beat on the floor, along with lower jaw not lining up and balance going, I won't make it to 70 years old! I'm not mad—just upset. Upset that I couldn't tell the judge I had proof of everything down to co-signing for loans on the house, motorcycle, and camper—that I had witnesses and medical records that were not allowed in court to prove my case. When the law can't help you using the 215 Ruling as the reason, you write about it and tell the world!

As a people and as a society, we can not be afraid to find and enact the solutions that will deal with those members of the human race who are out of control, threatening, beating, and acting beyond reason. Although it may push anyone of us to the limit of our religious beliefs, we are morally obligated to address deviant human behavior. No one in a civilized community is above the law for resolution and closure!

As I reflect on my journal entry of June 22, 1996, I am reminded that one of my affirmations to help me through hard times was as follows: "A *ship that always sails backward never sees the sunset.*" Since I have been able to share my story with you, I am no longer sailing backward; rather I'm moving forward, and, therefore, expecting to see many, many sunsets again!

So as I close from telling my story, it is my hope that someone else will benefit from what I endured and will not have to experience anything like that horrible nightmare. I've cried "My Last Tears." Thanks for listening, and God bless you all.

Love,

Deborah Brisco-Harvey

PART VII - FYI / Available Resources

(Taken from printed material)

Signs of an Abusive Relationship

YOU COULD BE IN AN ABUSIVE RELATIONSHIP IF . . .

- You constantly worry about your partner's moods and change your behavior to deal with them
- You feel like you are walking on eggshells
- Your partner seems like two different people
- You are afraid of your partner's temper
- You don't see family or friends to avoid your partner's jealousy or anger
- Your partner wants to control where you go and what you do
- Your partner constantly accuses you of having affairs
- Your partner wants to take all of your money or to need him for his money
- Your partner ridicules, puts down or humiliates you
- You find yourself doing what he wants to avoid his anger
- Your partner blames you for all the failures in the relationship
- Your partner says it's all your fault he's in pain
- He screams at you, throws things, breaks or steals your things
- He slaps, pulls, shoves, hits, kicks, burns, punches, or restrains you
- He threatens you with a weapon
- He claims he can't handle himself because of alcohol, drugs, or because he had an abusive childhood, etc.
- He forces you to have sex, hurts you during sex, or forces you to do sexual things against your will

* *

What is Domestic Violence?

Domestic violence occurs when a person uses a pattern of physical or psychological abuse, threats, intimidation, isolation or economic coercion to control another person in dating, family, or household relationship. While domestic violence is a wide-spread problem, there are many options available to help victims.

Obtaining An Order of Protection

An Order of Protection, which can be obtained in civil or criminal court, is a court order that can help victims with a variety of safety issues and concerns. If you were abused by a family member, significant other, or current or former household member, you might be eligible for an Order of Protection. An Order of Protection can also be obtained by a disabled adult who is abused by a caretaker. An Order of Protection can:

- Prohibit physical abuse, harassment, intimidation, or interference with personal liberty;

- Order the abuser to stay away from you and prohibit the abuser from going to your home, business or child's school;

- Require the abuser to attend counseling;

- Award you temporary custody of children and outline a visitation schedule;

- Prohibit the abuser from removing the children from the state or from the abused parent's care;

- Protect your personal belongings or property;

- Order the abuser to pay support or damages; and/or

- Order the abuser out of the house while under the influence of alcohol or drugs.

Stalking:

In 1992, the offense of stalking became a crime in Illinois. In order for the charge of stalking to be filed, the offender must transmit a threat to the victim of, or place the victim in reasonable fear of, immediate or future bodily harm, sexual assault, confinement or restraint. In addition to that threat, the offender must, at least twice, either follow the victim or place the victim under surveillance. If you think you are a victim of a stalking, contact your local police department immediately.

Getting Help From a Domestic Violence Agency

If you have experienced domestic violence, it is important to remember that victims do not cause abuse. Abusers are responsible for their own actions. If you have been abused, there are steps you can take to make things better. A domestic violence agency can help you understand what options are available, and help point you in the right direction. Domestic violence agencies can:

- Provide confidential counseling for you or your children.

- Provide emergency shelter or assistance in obtaining alternate permanent housing.

- Provide assistance and guidance in helping you deal with landlords, employers, schools and the court systems.

What Can You Do To Help Domestic Violence Victims?

If you know someone who is being abused, talk to them and offer support, encouragement and guidance; join them in court for moral support.

Contact a local domestic violence shelter and become a financial supporter, or see if you can help in other ways.

Educate people in your neighborhood, religious community or business about domestic violence and the needs of victims.

Encourage teachers and principals in your area to teach violence prevention and anger management as a regular part of their curriculum.

Call the State's Attorney's Office at (312) 443-5598 to arrange for a speaker on domestic violence for your group meeting.

Going to Court:
The Role of the State's Attorney

You may prosecute the abuser if his/her actions constitute a crime, such as striking you or damaging your property. To begin the process you must:

1. Contact the police and fill out a police report.

2. Take the police report to the local domestic violence court as soon as possible to determine if you can obtain an Order of Protection, schedule a court hearing and begin the criminal process. If you qualify for an emergency Order of Protection, it will be issued on that same day. In order for your Order of Protection to remain in effect, you will have to return to court for future hearings.

3. It is important that you follow up by coming to court when needed. The assistant state's attorneys and victim-witness assistance staff will help guide you through the court process.

4. If the crime occurred in Chicago, your case will be heard at the Centralized Domestic Violence Court at 1340 South Michigan; bring your police report and plan to arrive between 8:30 and 11:30 a.m. on any weekday (except court holidays) to initiate court action. Call (312) 341-2743 for further information.

5. If the crime occurred in a Cook County suburb, contact the State's Attorney's Office in your district for more information. Each suburban district hears domestic violence cases on a different schedule; call for further information:

    Skokie - (708) 470-7300, TDD: 470-5970
    Rolling Meadows - (708) 818-2326, TDD: 818-2838
    Maywood - (708) 865-6080, TDD: 865-6402
    Bridgeview - (708) 974-6250, TDD: 974-6380
    Markham - (708) 210-4060, TDD: 210-4190

Domestic Violence Hotlines

CHICAGO (312 Area Code)
Access Living (People with disabilities)		226-5900
	TDD:	226-1687
*Apna Ghar (North)		334-4663
*Family Rescue (North)		375-8400
	TDD:	375-8774
*Greenhouse (North)		278-4566
	TDD:	278-4114
Horizons (Lesbian and Gay)		871-2273
*House of Good Shepherd (North)		935-3434
Mujeres Latinas En Accion (South)		226-1544

Polish Welfare Association (North & South)	254-4444
Rainbow House/Arco Iris (South)	762-6611
TDD:	762-7038
Southwest Women Working Together	436-0550
TDD:	436-8243
TIA's Women's Program (South)	847-5602
TDD:	847-7121
Uptown Hull House (North)	561-3500
TDD:	561-6119

SUBURBAN COOK COUNTY (708 Area Code)

*Constance Morris House (West)	482-5254
TDD:	485-5257
*Crisis Center for South Suburbia	429-SAFE
TDD:	429-7284
*Evanston Shelter (North)	864-8780
LifeSpan (North)	824-4454
TDD:	824-0189
*South Suburban Family Shelter	335-3028
TDD:	429-7284

Elder Abuse:
State of Illinois Hotline	(800) 252-8966
State's Attorney's Hotline	(312) 443-4377

(* Denotes shelter facility)

LEGAL ASSISTANCE AGENCIES

Chicago Bar Association/ YWCA Battered Women's Program	(312) 372-4105
Cook County Legal Assistance Foundation (Suburbs only)	(708) 524-2600
Legal Assistance Foundation (Chicago only)	(312) 341-1070
Life Span's Center for Legal Services	(708) 824-0382
Pro Bono Advocates	(312) 906-8010

STATE'S ATTORNEY'S OFFICE

Victim-Witness Unit	(312) 890-7200
TDD:	890-7494
Chicago's Domestic Violence Court	(312) 341-2743
TDD:	341-2840

(* Denotes shelter facility)

* *

Signs of a Battering Personality

Below is a list of behaviors that are seen in people who batter. The last four signs are almost always seen if the person is a batterer. If the person has several of the other behaviors (three or more) there is a strong potential for physical violence.

1. JEALOUSY: At the beginning of the relationship an abuser will always say that jealousy is a sign of love. Jealousy has nothing to do with love; it's a sign of insecurity and possessiveness. A batterer will question you about who you talk to, accuse you of flirting, or be jealous of time you spend with family and friends, or children. As the jealousy progresses, the abuser may call frequently during the day or drop by unexpectedly to check up on you. The abuser may insist that you not work or check the car mileage or ask friends to watch you.

2. CONTROLLING BEHAVIOR: At first, the batterer will say that this behavior comes from concern about your safety, your need to make good decisions. The abuser will be angry if you are late coming home, and may question you closely about where you went or who you talked to. As this behavior gets worse, you may not be allowed to make decisions about the house, your clothing, going out. The abuser may keep all of the money or make you ask permission to leave the house.

3. QUICK INVOLVEMENT: Many survivors of domestic violence dated or knew the abuser for less than six months before they were living together. The abuser comes on like a whirl-wind claiming "love at first sight," and the person may tell you such flattering things as "you're the only person I could ever talk to" or "I've never loved anyone like this before."

4. UNREALISTIC EXPECTATIONS: A batterer may be very dependent on you to get all needs met. Your are expected to be the perfect lover and friend. The abuser may say things like "I'm all you need and you're all I need." You are expected to take care of everything emotionally and in the home.

5. ISLOLATION: A batterer will try to cut you off from all resources. If you have friends, you're either a slut or you're really straight. People who are your supports are accused of causing trouble. You may not be able to use the phone or car or go to school or work.

6. <u>BLAMES OTHERS FOR PROBLEMS</u>: Your abuser's problems are justified by saying "people are out to get me." The abuser may blame problems on you, and claim that you are at fault for everything that goes wrong.

7. <u>BLAMES OTHERS FOR FEELINGS</u>: The abuser will say "you make me mad," "you're hurting me by not doing what I ask," "I can't help being mad." Every person makes decisions about how to feel and think, but an abuser will use those feelings to manipulate you.

8. <u>HYPERSENSITIVITY</u>: The abuser is easily insulted, claims hurt feelings when really mad, or takes the slightest setbacks as personal attacks. The abuser will rant and rave about the injustice of things that have happened.

9. <u>CRUELTY TO CHILDREN OR TO ANIMALS</u>: This person may punish animals brutally or be insensitive to their pain and suffering. The person may expect children to do things beyond their ability or tease them until they cry.

10. <u>PLAYFUL USE OF FORCE IN SEX</u>: This person may like to throw you down and hold you down during sex, or act out fantasies where your are helpless. The abuser is letting you know that the idea of rape is exciting. The abuser may show little or no concern about whether you want to have sex and use sulking or manipulation to get you to comply. The abuser may start to have sex with you while you are sleeping or demand sex while you are ill or tired or right after an assault.

11. <u>VERBAL ABUSE</u>: In addition to saying things that are cruel or hurtful, this person may degrade you, curse you, or run down your accomplishments. The abuser will tell you that you are stupid and unable to function alone.

12. <u>TWO VERY DIFFERENT PERSONALITIES</u>: You may be confused by the batterer's sudden changes of mood. One minute the person is nice, and the next minute explosive or very sad. This does not indicate some special kind of mental problem or that the person is "crazy."

13. <u>PAST BATTERING</u>: You may find out that the abuser has hit past lovers, but claim that they provoked or exaggerated it. A batterer will assault any person they are with. Situational circumstances do not make a person better.

14. <u>THREATS OF VIOLENCE</u>: "I'll slap your mouth off," "I'll kill you" are examples of threats. Threats can also be non-verbal like angry gesturing, clenched fists, or standing in a doorway during an argument. The abuser may threaten to come out for you at work or with your family.

15. <u>BREAKING OR STRIKING OBJECTS</u>: This behavior is used as punishment and used to terrorize you. The batterer will select specific items of personal worth to destroy. The person may strike tables or walls or throw objects near you.

16. <u>ANY FORCE DURING AN ARGUMENT</u>: This may involve holding you down, restraining you from leaving the room, any pushing or shoving. Any physical assault is considered battering.

If you're going through any of this, please contact someone from following pages for help. Nobody has to live like that. I know.

* *

Below is a sample of a Victim Rights Sheet, which should be available through your local police department.

Illinois Domestic Violence Act: Rights of Victims

Battery is a crime. Any person who hits, chokes, kicks, threatens, harasses or interferes with the personal liberty of another family or household member (*except reasonable parental discipline*) has broken the law.

Victims of domestic violence have the right to:
• be protected from further abuse, neglect and exploitation
• press criminal charges against the abuser. (*NOTE: Jail is **not** the only outcome if the abuser is found guilty.*)
The court may now issue an **Order of Protection** on the victim's behalf. The Order can"
• Protect from further abuse, neglect and exploitation*
• bar the violent party temporarily from the home*
• order the offender to pay support, medical costs and legal expenses
• award child custody and prohibit child snatching
• prohibit destruction of victim's property
• require offender to undergo counseling
• offer other relief as appropriate.

To obtain an **Order of Protection:**
1) ask your attorney to file a petition in civil court; or

2) request an **Order of Protection** in conjunction with divorce proceedings; or

3) request an **Order of Protection** during the course of criminal prosecution.

An Order can be requested on your own behalf and / or on behalf of a child or an incapacitated adult.

Law enforcement officers are to use all reasonable means to prevent further abuse, including:
- arranging for the victim's transportation to a medical facility or safe shelter; and / or accompanying the victim back to the residence to get belongings
- arresting the abuser where appropriate, and completing a police report on all bona fide incidents
- advising the victim of his / her rights and the importance of preserving evidence.

If the abuser has left the scene and has not been arrested, you can still press criminal charges by going to your local State's Attorney's office during normal business hours.

To contact the domestic violence program in your area, see the last two pages of this book. For other help, contact: _____

*Violation of these provisions is a Class A misdemeanor.

Officer's Name	Department	Date	Badge No.

* *

Organizations to Contact

Illinois Coalition Against Domestic Violence
730 East Vine Street, Room 109 ~ Springfield, IL 62703 ~ 217/789-2830

Below is a list of ICADV members. There may be other domestic violence services in your area. Check the telephone yellow pages under "Social Services" or call your local police department for assistance.

ALEDO
Mercer County CADV
309 / 582-7233

ALTON
Oasis Women's Center
618 / 465-1978

AURORA
Mutual Ground
708 / 897-0080

BELLEVILLE
Women's Crisis Center of Metro
East
618 / 235-0892
618 / 398-8540

BLOOMINGTON
Countering Domestic Violence
309 / 827-7070

CAIRO
Cairo Women's Shelter
618 / 734-4357
618 / 524-4357

CANTON
Fulton County Women's Crisis
Service
309 / 647-8311

CARBONDALE
Women's Center
618 / 529-2324
618 / 997-2277

CENTRALIA
People Against Violent
Environments
618 / 533-7233
800 / 924-8444

CHARLESTON
Coalition Against Domestic
Violence
217 / 345-4300
217 / 235-4300

CHICAGO
Chicago Abused Women Coalition
312 / 278-4566

Family Rescue
312 / 375-8400

Mujeres Latinas en Accion
312 / 226-1544

Neopolitan Lighthouse
312 / 638-0227
312 / 638-0228 (TDD)

United Charities of Chicago-Family
Options
312 / 436-2400 (day phone)

DANVILLE
Danville YWCA Women's Shelter
217 / 443-5566

DE KALB
Safe Passage
815 / 756-5228

ELGIN
Community Crisis Center
708 / 697-2380 (Voice / TDD)

FREEPORT
VOICES...Breaking the Silence
815 / 235-1641
815 / 777-3680

GALESBURG
Knox County CADV
309 / 343-7233

GLEN ELLYN
Family Shelter Service
708 / 469-5650
708 / 260-7569 (TDD, 9-3, M-F)

HARRISBURG
Anna Bixby Women's Center
618 / 252-8389
800 / 421-8456

HAZEL CREST
South Suburban Family Shelter
708 / 335-3028

JOLIET
Groundwork
815 / 729-1228
815 / 722-3344

KANKAKEE
Kankakee County Coalition Against
Domestic Violence / Harbor House
815 / 932-5800

MACOMB
Quad County Coalition
Against Domestic Violence
309 / 837-5555

MOLINE
Family Resources - Domestic
Violence Advocacy Program
309 / 797-1777

OAK PARK
Sarah's Inn
708 / 386-4225
708 / 386-3687 (TDD, 9-5, M-S)

OLNEY
Stopping Woman Abuse Now, Inc.
618 / 392-3556

PEORIA
Center for Prevention of Abuse
309 / 691-4111

PRINCETON
Freedom House
815 / 875-8233
309 / 853-4961

QUINCY
Quanada
217 / 222-2873
217 / 285-6119

ROCHELLE
HOPE
815 / 562-8890

ROCKFORD
PHASE / WAVE
815 / 962-6102

STERLING
COVE
815 / 626-7277
815 / 288-1011
815 / 772-7959

STREATOR
Alternatives to Domestic Violence
815 / 673-1555
800 / 892-3375

SUMMIT
Des Plaines Valley Community
Center
708 / 485-5254
708 / 485-5857

TINLEY PARK
Crisis Center for South Suburbia
708 / 429-7233
708 / 429-7284 (TDD)

WAUKEGAN
A Safe Place / Lake County Crisis
 Center
708 / 249-4450

* *